THE
FIFTY GREATEST GOLFERS

The Fifty Greatest Post-War Golfers
From Around The World

Selected by

Peter Alliss
Peter Dobereiner
Mark McCormack
Arnold Palmer

GALLERY BOOKS
An Imprint of W. H. Smith Publishers Inc.
112 Madison Avenue
New York City 10016

First published in Great Britain in 1985 by
Kingswood/Quixote under the title
The Lord's Taverners Fifty Greatest Golfers

This edition published in 1987 by Gallery Books
An imprint of W. H. Smith Publishers Inc.
112 Madson Avenue, New York, New York 10016

By arrangement with Octopus Books Limited

Reprinted 1988

ISBN 0–8317–0023–8

Printed in Hong Kong

CONTENTS

INTRODUCTION

I was most flattered when asked by The Lord's Taverners to chair a panel of experts to pick the 50 leading golfers of the world since the end of World War II. My initial task was to surround myself with an expert team which would show no fear or favour. My first choice was the very respected golf correspondent of *The Observer*, Peter Dobereiner. The reason that Peter was the first to come to mind was his keen eye for detail, his enormous experience – after all, he has covered golf tournaments throughout the length and breadth of the world – and because he was someone who would fully appreciate that the names in this book would be those not only renowned for their golfing prowess but also for their great contribution to the game of golf itself.

Mark McCormack, the American lawyer, author, entrepreneur and business expert extraordinaire, was my next choice. Again because of his undoubted golfing knowledge, allied to a keen lawyer's brain and a sense of fair play.

Who, I wondered, would be our fourth? Then it came to me in a blinding flash, perhaps the greatest golfing cavalier since those far off days of Walter Hagen: who else but the one and only Arnold Palmer? Would they take part, I wondered? Out went the cables and before you could say 'The honourable company of Edinburgh Golfers' back came three 'yeses'. We were off and running.

Now I'm sure most of you at some time or other in your lives have heard that excellent long-running radio programme hosted by the legendary Roy Plomley, *Desert Island Discs*. All you have to do is pick eight records to take with you to some deserted isle which will keep you happy and contented until rescue comes. No easy task. How often have I driven up and down the world's motorways and tried to pick my eight records! You know, to this day, I'm still not one hundred percent sure which ones they would be; and so it was as we sat down on this assignment. It was a piece of cake getting to 40, 42, even 44, then suddenly there were at least 25 runners for just six places. We met, compared notes, went away, thought, argued, discussed, thought again – for one of the main problems was that the '50 Greats' were not just to be picked on results alone, but points like how they had played the game, their attitude towards international competitions and their willingness to support the game of golf in far-flung lands when, perhaps, money was not the be-all and end-all of everything also had to be taken into consideration. In other words, apart from their enormous skills, what had been their true contribution to golf?

I am sure as you go through our list you will find some choices that you disagree with, but you must remember that some of the newer names in the world of golf have not, in an overall way, been around long enough to have made a major contribution to the game. Their time will surely come and their names will be there when the next book of golfing greats is compiled.

My thanks then to my fellow panellists, Peter, Mark and Arnold. I can't, hand on heart, say that we never disagreed, but I can assure you that the final results in this book were quite unanimous.

I would also like to pay tribute to Mike Francis, Ivan Rose, Rodger Towers and Ron Wootton, who have done such a superb job in their various styles of capturing the flow, movement and character of the players.

All that remains is for me to wish you many years of happy golf — and hope you enjoy the forthcoming pages.

Peter Alliss

THE SELECTORS

PETER ALLISS

b. Berlin, Germany, 28 February, 1931

The name of Peter Alliss would appear on many people's list of the top fifty golfers since the war. Son of Percy Alliss, one of the foremost British professionals between the wars, Peter lost no time in following in his father's footsteps, turning pro in 1946 at the age of 15 and playing in his first Open a year later. Although he never succeeded in winning any of the major championships, his victory tally in European tournaments was impressive: no less than twenty wins between 1954 and 1969, including the Italian, Spanish and Portuguese Opens in the space of three weeks in 1958. His first appearance in the Ryder Cup was in 1953, and with the single exception of 1955 he represented Great Britain and Ireland in the event until 1969. Peter Alliss' retirement from international golf at the early age of 38 ('I began to twitch on the short putts') has led to a successful triple career as a broadcaster, writer and golf course design consultant. As a TV commentator he is known to millions of viewers in America, Canada and Australia as well as the UK, and on programmes such as the popular 'Pro-Celebrity' series and 'Around with Alliss' his cheerful and informed presentation has helped to convert many non-golfers to the sport. His writing credits include the series of *Bedside Golf* books, *Peter Alliss – An Autobiography*, *The Who's Who of Golf* and a novel published in 1983, *The Duke*. Among the golf courses he has designed and constructed in partnership with David Thomas is the Belfry at Sutton Coldfield, national headquarters of the PGA and a Ryder Cup venue.

ARNOLD PALMER

b. Latrobe, Pennsylvania, 10 September, 1929

No-one has captured the golfing public's imagination or commanded its affection and respect more than Arnold Palmer. Powerful, flamboyant, good-humoured and a born entertainer, he was unquestionably one of the greatest and most exciting golfers of all time and more than anyone else responsible for turning golf into a mass spectator sport. He first came into prominence in 1954 when he won the US Amateur championship in Detroit. He turned professional shortly afterwards, winning the Canadian Open in 1955 and the first of his major championships, the US Masters, three years later. In 1960 he won the US Open (beating a young amateur by the name of Jack Nicklaus into second place) and in the following year registered the first of two successive victories in the British Open – his participation in the event helping to restore it to its position as one of the world's major championships. During the sixties, when he was voted 'The Athlete of the Decade' by American sports writers, he chalked up another three victories in the US Masters, becoming the first to win the championship four times. In all he won 61 tournaments on the American professional circuit and a further 19 overseas. He was the first golfer to win a million dollars in official prize money and, in keeping with his image as an American hero, the first to fly his own plane to tournaments. Since 1979 he has played with great success on the Seniors Tour and he is the resident host of the Bay Hill Classic, staged each year on his own golf course at Orlando, Florida.

PETER DOBEREINER

b. London, England, 3 November, 1925

Since becoming golf correspondent of *The Observer* in 1965, Peter Dobereiner has written three million words and flown one million miles in pursuit of his subject. There was a time though when his career seemed to be travelling in quite a different direction. After briefly reading law at Oxford he volunteered for wartime service in the Royal Navy as a pilot. Then, with hostilities at an end, it was out to India where he ran a sugar refinery and associated factories involved in the production of confectionary and pharmaceuticals – and where, with an inner eye to the future, he first became interested in golf. Following Independence in 1947 he returned to England and entered the world of journalism, graduating from provincial newspapers to the national *Daily Express* and *Daily Mail* where he was deputy features editor. In 1957 he joined *The Observer* as chief sports sub-editor and eight years later began the peripatetic occupation of golf correspondent. Now one of the most respected and widely read writers on the sport, his work is syndicated in newspapers and magazines throughout the golfing world. His ten books to date include a collection of *The Best of Dobereiner*, a guide to the rules of golf and, most recently, *The Book of Golf Disasters*; in the pipeline is a book about putting, written in collaboration with Arnold Palmer. In 1984 he received the Donald Ross Award from the American Society of Golf Course Architects for his contribution as a writer to the all-important subject of golf course design and construction.

MARK MCCORMACK

b. Chicago, Illinois, 6 November 1930

When he was six years old, Mark McCormack was knocked down by a car and suffered a fractured skull. With contact sports ruled out his father steered him towards golf and, as it turned out, a lifetime's passion and a business empire. He was educated at William and Mary, where he played number one on the college golf team, and at Yale Law School, before joining a leading Cleveland law firm. His golf was good enough for him to qualify for four US Amateur Championships, three British Amateurs and one US Open. This brought him into contact with some of the rising stars of the game; the rest is one of the great success stories of our time. Recruiting first Arnold Palmer then Gary Player and Jack Nicklaus under his management banner, McCormack almost single-handedly transformed golf into big business, creating spectacular rewards for his clients and himself. Today, 25 years on, his International Management Group is the largest and most influential sports marketing and merchandising organisation in the world, representing a host of sports celebrities (among other top talents) and events like Wimbledon and the British Open, as well as being a major producer of films and TV programming. Despite his ever widening activities, Mark McCormack has maintained his interest in golf. In the seventies he was publisher of the journal *Golf International* and since 1966 has produced the annual, *The World of Professional Golf*. His latest book, *What They Don't Teach You At Harvard Business School*, is predictably a best-seller on both sides of the Atlantic.

THE ARTISTS

Mike Francis, Ivan Rose, Rodger Towers and Ron Wootton first collaborated on the companion volume to this book, *The Fifty Greatest Cricketers*, their highly acclaimed paintings for the project later going on show in London in 1984.

Mike Francis' work has been regularly exhibited in London (at the Nicholas Treadwell Gallery) and in various collections throughout Europe and the USA. He lives and paints in Kent, though many of his commissions come from abroad where his work is in considerable demand. He is currently putting together his first one-man exhibition which is to be staged in England later in the year.

Ivan Rose began work at 15 as a model maker and served his apprenticeship with Rank Screen Advertising. Since then he has been a freelance artist and illustrator, lecturing from time to time at art schools in London and Perth, Scotland. He lives in Middlesex and his past sporting activities include fencing for Wembley and rowing for Twickenham. When he is not flexing his muscles, he likes to collect antiques.

Rodger Towers worked for ten years in London advertising agencies as a visualiser/typographer before going freelance in 1967. He spent six years designing record sleeves for EMI, then broadened out into other areas of illustration. Since then his work has been featured in scores of advertisements, and on countless film posters and book jackets. He is a keen yachtsman and is soon to embark on his first transatlantic voyage.

Ron Wootton spent his national service as the battalion artist. Back in civvy street he joined a leading London advertising agency as a visualiser/illustrator, and later became Creative Head of the department. He went freelance as an illustrator in 1967, and now has a studio in London and at his home in Kent. Among his favourite pastimes are sailing and painting watercolour landscapes, which he sells from the gallery at his home and through local exhibitions.

Bryan Organ is one of Britain's most distinguished portrait painters. He was born in Leicester in 1935 and studied at the Loughborough College of Art and Design and The Royal Academy School. His first one-man show in London was at the Redfern Gallery in 1967, since when there have been six others, as well as exhibitions in New York and Turin. Several of his paintings are in the National Portrait Gallery in London and others are in private collections in Germany, France, Italy, Canada, the USA and the UK. A list of his subjects reads like a miniature *Who's Who*: Malcolm Muggeridge, Sir Michael Tippett, Mary Quant, Nadia Nerina, Sir Roy Strong, Princess Margaret, Elton John, Lester Piggott, Harold Macmillan (Earl of Stockton), the Prince of Wales, Lady Diana Spencer (The Princess of Wales), Lord Denning, James Callaghan, the Duke of Edinburgh. Bryan Organ is a godfather to Prince Henry, second son of the Prince and Princess of Wales.

THE GOLFERS

ISAO AOKI

b. Abiko, Japan, 31 August, 1942

Japanese golfers are difficult to assess in comparative world terms because for the most part they concentrate their attentions on their own domestic golf circuit. As a rule their games do not travel well on the occasions that they do venture overseas, possibly because of the difficulty of adjusting to widely different environments and lifestyles. Aoki is an exception, a golfer who can step off an airliner in any part of the world and immediately demonstrate that he is a player of the highest class. In the narrowest professional terms, i.e. as a money earner, he is almost certainly the highest paid golfer in the world today. Aoki started in golf as a caddie, at the Abiko club in Chiba, where he was nicknamed the Tokyo Tower because he was well above average height. Like all boy caddies, he filled the hours of waiting for clients by chipping and putting near the caddie pen, acquiring the sensitive touch which is the hallmark of his game. A curious circumstance stamped his golf with its distinctive low-handed action. An American serviceman gave Aoki his set of clubs which, being full-sized, were far too long for the high school lad. Perforce he had to swing them in an exaggeratedly flat plane and wield the putter with the toe cocked into the air in the manner which has become familiar to golf watchers on every continent. Although he has not captured one of the four great classics of golf, virtually an impossibility for a player who follows a hit-and-run itinerary, Aoki can consider himself desperately unlucky not to have taken the US Open championship of 1980 at Baltusrol. He completed four rounds in 274, a score which would have won any other US Open in history. However, that was the year that Jack Nicklaus set record totals for all four rounds of the Open for 272. Aoki's best international performances were in winning the 1978 World Match-Play championship and the 1983 European Open championship. His reputation as a match-play specialist is further based on four victories in the Japanese match-play championship and sterling performances for Japan in the Goldwin Cup matches against the United States. His one victory in the United States was the 1983 Hawaiian Open where he pitched 128 yards from the rough straight into the hole at the 72nd for the eagle which gave him the title by one stroke. On his home circuit Aoki has won 40 tournaments.

Mike Francis

SEVERIANO BALLESTEROS

b. Santander, Spain, 9 April, 1957

There is always discussion among golfers about who might be the greatest player in the world at any given moment. There are so many different methods of measuring a player's status: money winnings, tournament victories, stroke average, major championships and so on. Even before he won the Open championship at Royal Lytham in 1979 there was a considerable body of informed golfing opinion which held that Severiano Ballesteros was number one. By 1983 all arguments were silenced; by every yardstick the dashing Spaniard was top man on the totem pole. It had been a long and turbulent journey for the former caddie who taught himself to play golf with a hand-me-down 3-iron. He was the youngest of four brothers, all professional golfers, but that did not mean he was given extensive tuition. He was a loner, sneaking off onto the forbidden territory of the Santander golf course at the age of 8 to discover the joys and frustrations of golf under the cover of dusk. That was real golf, a vast improvement on his apprenticeship of hitting stones on the beach and around the family farm. Perhaps the most valuable aspect of that early initiation was that there was no-one around to indoctrinate him into the cautious habits of playing safe and swinging within himself. He played with the logic of innocence, hitting the ball as hard as he could and aiming straight at the target on every shot, regardless of the dangers. He also gambled with the other caddie boys, pitching and chipping and putting for *pesetas*, and always for more than he could afford to lose. As he grew into a tall, well set up youth, he emerged as the most exciting golfer of the day, a huge hitter who performed prodigies of recovery from the inevitable wild shots. Most of all, though, he had exquisite finesse in his hands for the touch shots on and around the green. All he needed was to refine and restrain the raw talent of his long game and that came through hard experience. Unlike most golfers from a similar background, whose ambitions are limited by dreams of modest comfort and security, Ballesteros was driven by an obsession to beat the world. He thus had the two elements for success, the game and the desire, and he took golf by storm. He particularly relished beating Americans, not because he disliked them but because he recognised that they were the best players and therefore worthy scalps to be taken. Having fought many bitter battles on his way to the top, his uncompromising nature has mellowed and he has become the most gracious, if still supremely competitive, of champions.

Open champion 1979, 1984. Masters champion 1980, 1983. World Cup (with Manuel Pinero) 1976, (with Antonio Garrido) 1977. Winner of the championships of ten different nations.

Ivan Rose

TOMMY BOLT

b. Haworth, Oklahoma, 31 March, 1918

The primary concern of nature is balance. For every force there is an equal and opposite reaction. For every predatory fox there must be a nourishing rabbit. For every creature breathing oxygen and exhaling nitrogen there must be a plant absorbing nitrogen and photosynthesising fresh oxygen. Likewise with people, balance is nature's objective. If nature endows someone with the precious gift of artistry it balances the account by adding an artistic temperament. Hence Tommy Bolt, one of the most gifted stroke-makers of the modern era and one of the most volcanic personalities the game has seen. As with most temperamental golfers, Bolt's outbursts were directed against himself for the most part, since they were expressions of the sensitivity which was the basis of his golfing genius. In his hands a golf club took on the characteristics of a magic wand. He had the vision to see shots which would not occur to his contemporaries and he also had the ability to fashion the strokes to achieve his object. Golf, as everyone knows, abhors a perfectionist and inevitably some of Bolt's shots fell short of his ambition. When they fell short into water, or some equally aggravating lie, Bolt was temperamentally incapable of hanging onto the club – or onto his tongue. It did not take long for him to earn the obvious nickname of Thunder Bolt and his fiery temper cost him dearly in fines. As a golfer he resembled the little girl who had a little curl right in the middle of her forehead; when he was good he was very, very good but when he was bad he was horrid. He was very, very good often enough to win 14 PGA tournaments and in 1958 at Southern Hills his gigantic potential was fulfilled when, in a searing heatwave, he fashioned closing rounds of 69, 72 to win the US Open championship. Wherever golf was played people swapped Tommy Bolt stories, many of them apocryphal although there were enough authenticated ones to sate the most lurid imagination, and Bolt did nothing to reverse the process. Notoriety was good for business, a lesson that professional tennis players were later to exploit. It was only golf that set the torch to Bolt's short fuse. Off the course his generosity and rough-hewn charm won him many friends.

US Open champion 1958. World Seniors champion 1969.

Ron Wootton

MICHAEL BONALLACK

b. Chigwell, Essex, 31 December, 1934

In the days before professional golf was considered to be a suitable vocation for gentlemen, i.e. before it was possible to earn fortunes from the game, the best amateurs stayed amateur and they were every bit as accomplished as the finest pros. Indeed, in the case of Bobby Jones, he was incomparably better than the finest pros. Michael Bonallack was probably the last British amateur to fall into this category, although at the time he always maintained, in the clipped, self-mocking tone which suggested that his school tie might with benefit be loosened, that he never contemplated turning pro on the grounds that he and his family would surely starve. That view was not shared by those who fell victim to his fighting spirit and wizardry with the putter, nor by those who watched his remarkable run of success. Purists could not give unmitigated approval of his swing, which frequently involved bouncing the shaft on his left shoulder at the top or, more accurately, over the top, and he was not the straightest of players with the long clubs. But his short game, and especially his putting, backed by an indomitable temperament, pulled him through and made him equally formidable at stroke-play and as a match-player. From the time he won the British Boys' championship in 1952 Bonallack went from strength to strength and won every honour of note in British amateur golf, most of them several times over, and he represented England more often, and to better effect, than any player in history. He was not an exact contemporary of the great Irish amateur, Joe Carr, who was at his best before Bonallack reached his prime, but their careers overlapped and their battles provided some of the most stirring matches of the time. Although he won the Amateur championship five times, three in a row from 1968, and the English Amateur a record five times, competed in the Masters and was a stalwart of innumerable international matches, it was not until 1971 that he achieved his greatest ambition when he captained the Walker Cup team to victory at St Andrews. He was awarded the OBE for his services to golf that year. As his increasing business activities began to curtail his opportunities for competitive play, Bonallack began to play an increasing part in the administration of golf, culminating in his appointment as secretary of the Royal and Ancient golf club of St Andrews. In this capacity he was responsible for mounting the 1984 Open championship at St Andrews, which proved to be the most successful championship in its 113 year history.

Amateur champion 1961, 1965, 1968, 1969, 1970. English Amateur champion 1962, 1963, 1965, 1967, 1968. English Amateur stroke-play champion 1964, 1968, 1971. Member of nine Walker Cup teams, captain 1969, 1971. Member of seven Eisenhower Trophy teams, captain 1968, 1970, 1972.

Ivan Rose

JULIUS BOROS

b. Fairfield, Connecticut, 3 March, 1920

For the novice golfer who is struggling to master the frustrating complexities of golf technique it is sometimes possible to observe one swing by a great player, such as Gene Sarazen, and to comprehend the secret in a flash of revelation. Of course, of course! You simply turn everything this way and then turn it all back the other way and the ball pings off the club-face straight and far. How obvious – and how foolish of me to clog my mind with esoteric details about pronating the wrists and elongating the left thumb. Julius Boros was a splendid example for the novice in many ways but his swing revealed no mysteries. It compounded the mystery, one of the great enigmas of modern golf. It is quite true that Bobby Jones, who knew as much about golf as anyone and wrote about it better than anyone, said: 'It is impossible to swing the golf club too slowly.' But Boros swung so slowly that the onlooker wondered how he managed to move the ball forward at all. With the languid tempo of a man stretching after a deep sleep, Boros turned away and then reversed direction at the same lazy pace. His action looked like a slow-motion replay of a golf swing, apparently defying Einstein's law of relativity which decrees that the speed of the object (ball) is proportionate to the mass of the subject (club-head) and the square of its speed. Even the square of Boros's club-head speed, you imagined, would be pretty sluggish. Therein lay the art that concealed art. The watcher was mesmerised by the effortless swing and failed to observe, because the human eye could not follow it, the acceleration of the club-head. In terms of energy-conversion the swing of Julius Boros was probably the most efficient ever seen in championship golf. It was an extension of his personality because Boros lived at half speed. Walking, talking, even tying up his shoelaces, every action was a study in deliberation, the very personification of *festina lente*. He turned pro in 1950 and maintained that he should have won his first tournament, the US Open at Merion. A 77 in the third round relegated him to ninth place but he earned the rare distinction of breaking his tournament duck with a classic victory when he won the US Open at Dallas two years later. Eleven years later he repeated that triumph, winning the national championship at Brookline and taking a third major championship, the US PGA at San Antonio, at the age of 48.

US Open champion 1952, 1963. PGA champion 1968.
Member of four Ryder Cup teams. Won Canada Cup (with
Jim Turnesa) 1952 and World Cup (with Lee Trevino) 1968.

Mike Francis

JACK BURKE

b. Fort Worth, Texas, 29 January, 1923

Racing men refer to horses for courses and every keen punter knows which thoroughbreds like heavy underfoot conditions and which prefer firm going. Golf, too, has its thoroughbreds and, like their equine counterparts, the tournament professionals have their preferences for different courses and also the conditions which suit them best. Thus Tom Watson is particularly associated with links courses, Johnny Miller with desert courses and Severiano Ballesteros has developed a special affinity for the Augusta National club. It would probably be overloading the truth to nominate specific golfers as players who enjoyed tackling turbulent conditions. Perhaps it would be nearer the mark to say that they welcomed rough weather because they knew it would destroy their rivals and enable them to profit from their own special talents for controlling the ball. Arnold Palmer and Christy O'Connor immediately come to mind, followed after a moment of reflection by the stocky Texan Jack Burke. A hand injury curtailed Burke's career to a meagre ten years of full time competitive golf but it was a decade of concentrated success. He turned pro at the age of 17 and, after war service with the US Marine Corps, held a number of club appointments. He was thus a veteran in sporting terms when he joined the circuit in the early fifties. He won 15 tournaments, four in a row in 1956, including the Masters and the PGA championship. His record in the Ryder Cup matches was outstanding, unbeaten in his first three series and losing that proud record only on his fourth appearance when he was beaten by Peter Mills in their singles match. To add insult to that injury he was captain that year, 1957, at Lindrick and that was the only occasion since the war that the American team suffered a defeat. The American PGA gave him his eagerly awaited chance to avenge that reverse by appointing him the non-playing captain in 1973 when a fine victory by the Americans erased the blot on the Burke escutcheon. Burke's mastery in the wind was probably seen to its best advantage during the 1952 Masters when it blew harder than at any time in the history of the tournament. His closing 69 was the only score below 70 in the last two rounds. After his retirement from the competitive scene Burke devoted himself to running the Champions Club in Houston in partnership with Jimmy Demaret.

Masters champion 1956. US PGA champion 1956. Member of four Ryder Cup teams, playing captain 1957 and non-playing captain 1973.

Rodger Towers

BILLY CASPER

b. San Diego, California, 24 June, 1931

To the casual observer, and that word casual must be stressed, the success of Billy Casper was slightly surprising. He became a tournament player at the rather advanced age of 24, during the era when Ben Hogan still commanded the most precise golf swing in the history of the game and when Arnold Palmer was enslaving a generation of fanatical disciples with his swashbuckling play. By comparison Casper's game looked insipid. He was overweight, his high and fading drives were modest in length and his iron play unremarkable. He had considerable early successes but they were dismissed as being the easy pickings of a steady golfer benefiting from the mistakes of the giants of golf. Casper's manager, a man more accustomed to operating in the sleazy ballyhoo of the Hollywood show business snake pit, tried to create an image for his man as the victim of allergies who had to live on the steaks of buffalo and rattlesnake. What the casual observer missed was that here was a player who had rationalised the game of golf as an enterprise in which the first requirement was to avoid mistakes from tee to green and who appreciated that the real business started when the putter was taken from the bag. Golf spectators mainly find putting to be a dull activity, offering nothing of the *sturm und drang* of massive drives and heroic recoveries. Casper, like Bobby Locke before him, recognised that golf tournaments were essentially putting contests; you somehow contrived to get the ball onto the green and then the real competition began. To the connoisseur Casper's putting stroke was a thing of rhythmic beauty. By any standards Casper was a superstar: twice US Open champion, Masters champion, 51 victories on the American PGA Tour and three more on the Senior Tour, five times winner of the Vardon Trophy for the season's lowest stroke average between 1960 and 1968, stalwart of eight Ryder Cup teams and non-playing captain in 1979. Throughout this intensive career Casper remained true to his priorities: he was first and foremost a devoted husband and father and disciple of the Mormon faith, secondly a professional golfer. He and his wife Shirley had eleven children, by natural issue and adoption. At the last count they had six grandchildren, and still counting. Towards the end of his active playing career Casper was the victim of a financial crash, when a massive investment in peach farming went horribly wrong, and at the same time, probably as a consequence, his game went to pot. In his first six tournaments of 1980 he hit 42 shots out of bounds; his drives were directed as much as 100 yards off line, and slicing horribly. Casper faced this twin crisis with resolution, dogged practice and a regime of mental rehabilitation which included splicing together tapes of his greatest triumphs to boost his confidence. As a result he had a resurgence of success on the Senior Tour, to the extent that he described the process as 'kicking over rocks and finding money underneath'.

US Open champion 1959, 1966. Masters champion 1970.
Member of eight Ryder Cup teams and non-playing captain
1979.

Ivan Rose

BOB CHARLES

b. Cartenton, New Zealand, 14 March, 1936

It is curious, considering the incidence of left-handers in sports such as tennis, cricket and boxing, that golf should have produced only one left-hander of genuine international stature. The explanation probably lies in the fact that the majority of youngsters take up the game with whatever equipment is available and this is predominantly cast-off right-handed clubs. Bob Charles never had to reverse his natural inclination because both his parents were keen left-handed golfers and they introduced him to their sinister game at the age of five. In fact he was naturally ambidextrous, using the right for one-handed operations such as writing but switching for two-handed actions. As a boy cricketer he bowled right-handed and batted left-handed. Charles went into banking after leaving college and worked as a teller for seven years, winning the New Zealand Open championship as an amateur in 1954 and playing for New Zealand in the first two Eisenhower Trophy tournaments. He turned pro in 1960 and brought to golf the logical and analytical mind of a banker. He reasoned that since he had schooled himself to become indisputably the finest putter in contemporary golf he must maximise his superiority on the greens. Everything else in golf must be preparation, a preliminary to the real game. He never strove for the heroic drive or the devastating thrust with the irons. His policy was to manoeuvre his ball as safely and economically as he could, keeping well clear of hazards, and then to build his score with devastating putting. Let the others try to overpower the course; he would stick with his short, straight hitting and have the last laugh on the greens. In an era of power golf it was a philosophy which required great strength of character and patience, which Charles possessed in ample quantities. He became the greatest left-hander in the history of the game, and by a long way, and one of the finest golfers of his day, regardless of style. The New Zealand professional championship of 1961 set him off on a winning career which culminated in his victory in the Open championship of 1963 at Royal Lytham and St Annes, where he beat the American Phil Rodgers by eight strokes in the last of the 36-hole play-offs. He was twice second in the Open and also runner-up in the US PGA championship. Charles campaigned with great success on the American PGA Tour and in 1969 won the world match-play championship.

Open champion 1963. New Zealand Open champion 1954, 1966, 1970.

Ron Wootton

NEIL COLES

b. London, 26 September, 1934

It is often remarked, and as frequently demonstrated, that it is impossible for an angry man to play golf. Neil Coles was blessed, and the word is selected with due consideration because his natural gift was the key to his success, with a personality of deep intensity. He was also born into an era when the professional golfer knew his place, accepting an occupational responsibility to be available at all times to attend every trifling request of the lordly members but otherwise to melt into the background, unseen and unheard. It was an unpropitious convention for a spectator sport, which thrives on flamboyance and extrovert behaviour in its stars, and Coles rather overdid the self-effacement, dressing in sober autumnal tints of such effective camouflage that he was virtually invisible on the golf course. At the same time he kept a firm lid on his volatile temperament, presenting a serene and impassive outward aspect while releasing the internal pressure in shots of great power and virtuosity, exploiting the principles which James Watt harnessed in his invention of the steam engine. There can be no doubt that Coles had the golf to beat the world and win the Open but it is another question whether this very private and home-loving man relished the hullabaloo and disruption which go with being the champion golfer. Besides, he had a strong phobia about air travel, which prevented him from seeking overseas titles. His style, therefore, was to concentrate on domestic tournaments, win as unobtrusively as he could, pocket the cheque and slip away quietly into the night. He pursued this programme with huge effect for thirty years, winning 30 tournaments and competing in eight Ryder Cup matches. As the very model of professional integrity and deportment, Coles was the obvious choice to guide the new European circuit when it was instituted in the early seventies. He served as chairman of the tournament committee, working closely with John Jacobs and then Ken Schofield, the executive directors of the fast growing organisation. His committee style resembled his golf, quiet and reserved but informed by an iron decisiveness. Much of the credit for the expansion of European professional golf must be given to Coles although he, typically, would disown it.

Member of eight Ryder Cup teams.

Ivan Rose

HENRY COTTON

b. Holmes Chapel, Cheshire, 26 January, 1907

When the Great Triumvirate of Harry Vardon, James Braid and J. H. Taylor reached the end of their reign, domination of professional golf passed to the United States and remained firmly in American hands until Henry Cotton determined to challenge and beat the world. He was a wilful schoolboy at Alleyn's when he decided to become a professional golfer, and he determined from the start that he must set his own standards and live by his own terms. He set himself a training programme of such rigour that his hands bled from practising into the night, but his obsessive drive for perfection paid off in 1934 at Sandwich when he built up a ten-stroke lead after two rounds and ended American supremacy of the Open championship by five strokes. At Carnoustie in 1937 he was opposed by the full strength of the visiting American Ryder Cup team but played what was regarded as one of the greatest rounds ever seen in the championship, a 71 in pelting rain over a waterlogged course, to take the title. War service with the RAF cheated him of his prime years, when he must surely have added to his championship tally. That opportunity had to wait until 1948 when he won his third championship, setting a record 66 for the Muirfield course. Cotton's outstanding record as a player was only one part of his gigantic contribution to golf and to his profession. By his example, and his adamant refusal to conform with the status of golf club servant which was the accepted lot of the professional golfer of his day, he emancipated the profession socially and raised the scale of rewards by his own acute business negotiations. He elevated both the standards and fees for teaching golf and had a great influence on the administration and growth of professional golf. He wrote fluently and prolifically about the game in a weekly newspaper column for thirty years, and in many books. Almost single-handed he raised the public consciousness and interest in his minority sport to the point where he could top the bill in variety performances with his golf act. As his playing career tapered off he devoted more and more time to the study and practice of golf architecture, designing several courses and building his monument, the beautiful courses at Penina, on the Algarve coast of Portugal, where he presided as the golfing legend in residence.

Open champion 1934, 1937, 1948. Member of three Ryder Cup teams, twice as captain.

Mike Francis

BEN CRENSHAW

b. Austin, Texas, 11 January, 1952

When Ben Crenshaw turned pro he had the kind of method which Sam Snead categorised as a 'flippy wristed college boy swing' and a respect bordering on reverence for the history, traditions and legends of golf. Snead and the other senior players all qualified as legends to Crenshaw and he listened attentively to their advice about how he must shorten his swing, and get that left wrist flat at the top of the swing, if he wanted to succeed on the pro circuit. Crenshaw had just qualified by winning the PGA school tournament by 12 strokes and had won the first professional tournament he entered, the Texas Open, but legends were not lightly be be disregarded. He diligently worked to acquire the approved professional method and it worked well enough to bring him ten tournament victories in ten years, not to mention putting him well on the way to his second million dollars in prize winnings. That was all very well but Crenshaw dreamed of treading in the footsteps of the giants of the past, of seeing his name engraved on trophies alongside those of the Morrises, Harry Vardon and Bobby Jones. He expressed his feelings with the words: 'I do not think I could go on living unless I felt that one day I might win the Open championship at St Andrews.' The intensity of Crenshaw's ambition, combined with his deep feelings about golf courses which he considered to be the cathedrals of the game, put him under enormous pressure in the classics, and at a considerable disadvantage in relation to rivals who regarded a major championship as just another tournament, on just another track. Crenshaw amassed an unenviable record of narrowly failing in the events he most wanted to win. He finished second in the Open championship twice, second in the Masters twice, and second in the US PGA championship. The papers started calling him the bridesmaid of golf and Crenshaw himself finally began to wonder if he would ever break through the psychological barrier which he had erected between himself and the classic titles. He pondered deeply on his problem and recalled his amateur days when he dominated college golf for three successive years. He decided to revert to the method which had brought him those satisfying honours. He switched back to his carefree, lashing style in the spring of 1984 and was immediately rewarded by winning the Masters. His victory was hailed as a triumph for the most effective putting stroke in American golf but there was more, much more, to it than that.

Masters champion 1984. Member of two Ryder Cup teams and one World Cup team.

Ivan Rose

JIMMY DEMARET

b. Houston, Texas, 24 May, 1910

Texas in the Depression years was the cradle of American professional golf, producing three players who were to challenge all standards and set a new conception of the game: Ben Hogan, Byron Nelson and Jimmy Demaret. Hogan rewrote the instruction books, Nelson the record books and Demaret contributed that indefinable quality of style, or what the Americans call class. Demaret was a nightclub singer and it says something of the times that when his boss sponsored him for a crack at the professional golf circuit he won six tournaments in a row, finishing with the Masters no less, and then quit to return to singing for fear that he might lose his job. He did indeed lose his job because this was 1940 and both singing and swinging had to be shelved for military service. Things were rather more secure after the war, largely because Nelson had stimulated public interest in pro golf during the only two years when he played full time tournament golf, 1944 and 1945, albeit winning 31 tournaments during that brief span. It was Demaret rather than Hogan who carried the banner for the Lone Star state in those immediate post-war years when the boys came marching home from the services. Demaret won his second Masters in 1947 and three years later he became the first golfer to win the Augusta classic three times when he made up seven strokes in the last six holes to beat the Australian Jim Ferrier. Most great golfers have an edge in some department of the game and in Demaret's case it was his wedge play. He was runner-up to Hogan in the 1948 US Open at Riviera, graciously acknowledging his friend's supremacy by dubbing the course 'Hogan's Alley'. However, Hogan had great respect and affection for Demaret and it was natural for them to team up for an unbeatable foursomes combination in the Ryder Cup matches of 1947 and 1951. Indeed, Demaret's record in the Ryder Cup matches, including two singles against the redoubtable Dai Rees, ranks among the best in the series for either of the opposing nations. It was therefore fitting, when Demaret and Jackie Burke created the Champions Club in Houston, that it should be selected for the 1967 match. A man of acute wit and charm, Demaret was one of the first, and best, golf commentators and was long associated with the popular television series 'Shell's Wonderful World of Golf'.

*Masters champion 1940, 1947, 1950. Member of three
Ryder Cup teams.*

Mike Francis

NICK FALDO

b. St Albans, Hertfordshire, 18 July, 1957

The inclusion of Nick Faldo in this gathering of illustrious golfers represented something of an act of faith on the part of the selectorial panel. True, it was no great gamble, for the young Englishman had given due notice of a great career even if he had not achieved the highest honours of the game. Faldo's introduction to golf was unconventional, in that he was a sports-mad schoolboy with considerable promise as a swimmer and athlete until he saw Jack Nicklaus on television. He concluded that the game was lucrative and, on the evidence of the television screen, not all that difficult. He acquired a club and some balls and put his theory to the test on his school playing fields, learning that there was more to this game than met the eye but being sufficiently encouraged to drop hints to his parents that a proper set of clubs would be an acceptable gift. The tall and athletic youngster made rapid progress, won the British Youths and English Amateur championships and turned pro late in 1976. The following year he won his first tournament and established himself as the most promising prospect British golf had seen since Tony Jacklin. He did not appreciate it at the time but he benefited enormously from the simultaneous arrival on the European Circuit of two other immensely gifted teenagers, Severiano Ballesteros and Sandy Lyle. They brought the best out of each other and, while the Spanish prodigy must be said to have had the best of those encounters, he certainly pulled Faldo along in his slipstream. One victory a year on the European circuit, with increasingly threatening performances, marked Faldo's progress for his first six years as a tournament professional and then in 1983, by which time he was competing regularly on the American PGA Tour, he really made his mark. Faldo was recruited as late replacement for the injured Greg Norman to provide the star element for the French Open championship and he won in devastating style, coming from behind to force his way into a play-off and then burning off the opposition with aggressive golf such as he had never before displayed. That win inspired him to a hat-trick of victories and a record five wins for the season. Early in the following year he won his first American PGA tournament, the Heritage Classic, to be recognised as an international player of the highest class.

Member of five Ryder Cup teams.

Rodger Towers

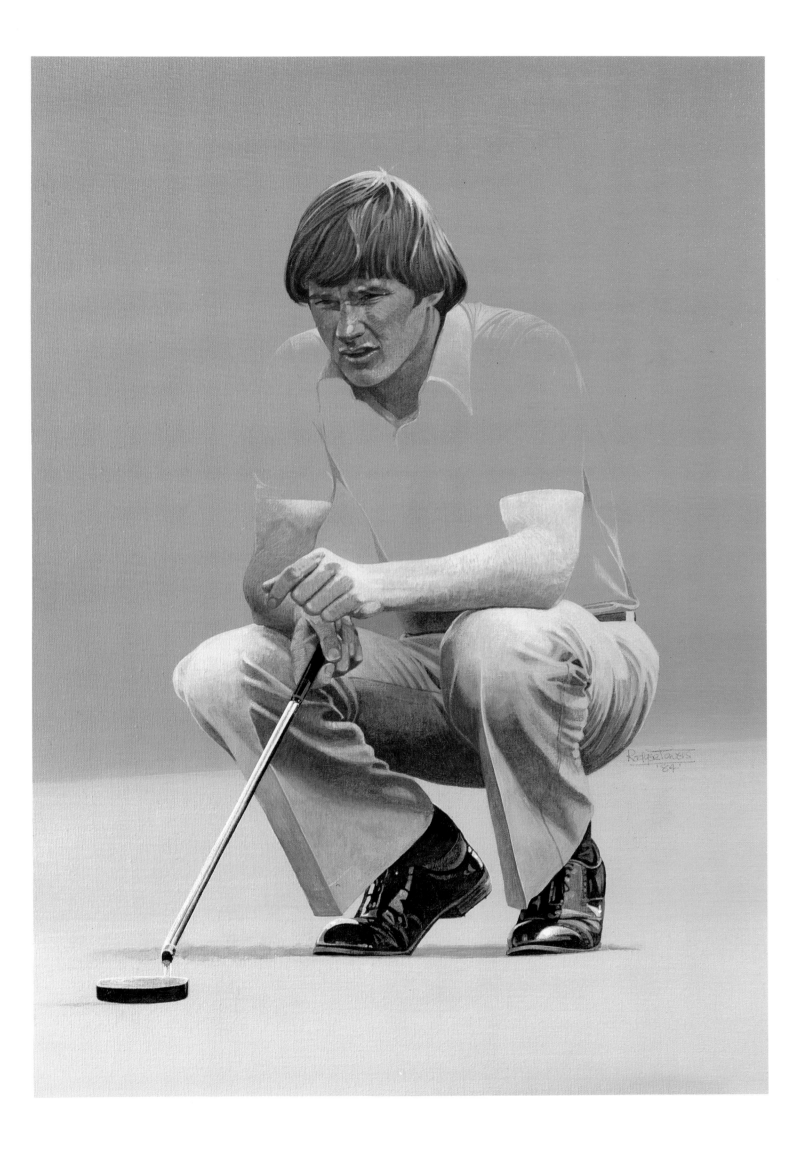

DOW FINSTERWALD

b. Athens, Ohio, 6 September, 1929

When Ben Hogan's glorious career came to an end there was intense and natural speculation about who the next Hogan might be. There were a number of promising candidates whose partisan supporters asserted confidently that Billy Casper, Ken Venturi or, with rather less assurance and therefore considerably less prescience, Arnold Palmer would claim the throne. There was also a faction for Dow Finsterwald, on the grounds that he was one of the most intelligent golfers around, a BA from Ohio University, who played smart golf. At that time, before Palmer and Severiano Ballesteros demonstrated that boldness on the links could be a positive virtue rather than a form of self-destruction, it was held to be axiomatic in professional golf that the first requirement for successful tournament play was to avoid risks. Finsterwald was the very personification of that school of thought. His paramount consideration was to keep the ball in play, aiming for the middle of the fairway and then the middle of the green. Then, with patience and a bit of luck, the scores would follow. As a way of golf it clearly embodied the virtue of consistency, as another practitioner of that golfing philosophy, Jack Nicklaus, was to demonstrate to such effect. It worked for Finsterwald, even if it never elevated him into the Hogan class. He quickly established himself as a solid performer after he turned pro in 1951 and won twelve tournaments between 1955 and 1963, winning the Vardon Trophy for the season's lowest stroke average in 1957. That was the year that he lost to Lionel Hebert in the final of the PGA championship, the last occasion that the title was contested at match-play. The following year Finsterwald returned a total of 276 at Havertown, Philadelphia, to win the first stroke-play PGA championship. In the Masters of 1962 Finsterwald's cautious golf put him in a tie with Arnold Palmer and Gary Player but on that occasion it was Palmer's aggressive style which prevailed in the play-off. That is not to infer that Finsterwald was more effective as a stroke-player (play-offs being close kin to match-play). In four Ryder Cup matches Finsterwald had the enviable record of nine victories to three losses. He was appointed to serve on the United States Golf Association's Rules of Golf Committee for the period 1979–81.

US PGA champion 1958. Member of four Ryder Cup teams.

Ivan Rose

RAYMOND FLOYD

b. Fort Bragg, North Carolina, 4 September, 1942

In the world of sport the word 'professional' has undergone a considerable transition as, indeed, has the word 'amateur'. Just as 'amateur' has lost its social distinction and come to mean almost a bungler, so 'professional' has risen in the world, out of the servants' hall of honest working-class toil into the drawing room of respectability and synonymous with excellence of workmanship. Raymond Floyd's story is much the same and today he is universally respected by his peers as the ultimate professional, the pros' pro. His is not a pretty swing, being laboured and stiff and containing a pronounced loop at the top. Purists might disapprove but Floyd's bank manager is more than satisfied with the action which by 1984 was well on the way to winning a third million dollars. Floyd's distinctive style is partly due to the fact that this tall and heavily built golfer has disproportionately short arms and has to play with clubs which are considerably longer than standard models. As a young professional fresh out of the University of North Carolina Floyd earned the reputation for being what the slang of the day termed a swinger, to the disapproval of the golfing greybeards, soured by the reflection that their own capacity for swinging had never enjoyed the opportunities offered by the age of permissiveness. Age always disapproves of youth and time duly took care of Floyd's youth. He matured into the solidest of citizens and the solidest of golfers, demonstrating an astonishing consistency. His first classic victory, the American PGA championship of 1969, may have been slightly premature in terms of his development and he profited on that occasion by the elimination of his two main challengers, Jack Nicklaus and Gary Player, by idiotic civil rights demonstrators who scared the wits out of them in the final round. However, Floyd went on to prove that he was by no means out of place in the company of the great champions when he won the 1976 Masters and repeated his PGA championship triumph in 1982. In twenty years of campaigning on the American PGA Tour and around the world he has averaged better than one victory a year, maintaining his status as one of the leading favourites every time he plays. He has been a stalwart of the American Ryder Cup team on five occasions.

PGA champion 1969, 1982. Masters champion 1976.

Ron Wootton

DOUG FORD

b. West Haven, Connecticut, 6 August, 1922

It is astonishing how many professional golfers distinguished themselves at other sports, often to the point of having to make a decision about which pursuit offered the best career prospects, before settling for the club and ball game. The world of professional golf could field accomplished teams for baseball, basketball and football and its ranks include one former tennis pro and a Lancashire League cricketer – and that is just the American PGA. Presumably all those previous sporting endeavours contributed to their success as golfers, if only to the extent of physical development and competitive hardening, but Doug Ford was unique in claiming a misspent youth in billiard saloons as an important formative influence on his golf. It developed his sensitive touch on the greens, he said. Certainly he was an outstanding putter and, although he was generally overshadowed by more illustrious contemporaries, he was more than a cut above the general run of working professionals. The highlights of Ford's career were the 1955 PGA championship, which was still contested at match-play in those days, and the Masters of 1957. In that PGA championship at Meadowbrook, Michigan, Ford's uncanny putting destroyed Cary Middlecoff by 4 and 3. Putting is more than half the battle at the Augusta National club, of course, with its fast and undulating greens and Ford again exploited his billiard cue touch to the fullest advantage, making up a three-stroke deficit on Sam Snead in the final round to win by three strokes. However, Ford's greatest virtue was not best illustrated by those two classic triumphs. His main strength was his consistency. Week after week his name was a fixture on the leader board. In twelve years he was never out of the top twenty, and mostly finished in the top ten. Ford won a total of 19 PGA tournaments and added to that tally when the Senior Tour began in 1980. That enterprise started rather too late for Ford, who was 58 by then and therefore at a disadvantage compared with the newly qualified 50-year-olds, but he still won himself a valuable supplement to his income. The Senior Tour provides an important service in demonstrating how golf should be played, all its members being vastly experienced. Ford's special contribution was a much needed reminder that fine golf can be played briskly, with the minimum of fuss and bother.

Masters champion 1957. US PGA champion 1955. Member of four Ryder Cup teams.

Rodger Towers

DOUG FORD
1955 U.S. P.G.A MATCHPLAY CHAMPION.
1957 MASTERS CHAMPION.

DAVID GRAHAM

b. Windsor, Australia, 23 May, 1946

Adherents of the Pilgrim's Progress school of thought, that triumph is the child of adversity, have a prime example in David Graham. Few players can have had to fight so hard and long against the cruelties of fate as the wiry Australian. Poverty and a broken home were just the first hurdles. When he did get a chance to take up golf it was with a set of cast-off left-handed clubs and it says much for his determined nature that he reached a fair standard with these unsuitable implements. His first venture as a club professional ended in bankruptcy and he had to labour at the bench as a club-maker in a factory to pay off his creditors. When he finally did start to make his mark as a tournament player he ran into further problems after a rash agreement with a rapacious manager. Far from being deterred, Graham doggedly followed his star and the hardening of his youth turned him into a formidable competitor. The game of golf can deliver some hard knocks but they were pinpricks to Graham after what he had survived. A most painstaking player, Graham put himself through a rigorous apprenticeship as a tournament golfer, competing in Europe and around the world until 1971 when he committed himself heart and soul to America and the American PGA Tour. His progress was steady if unspectacular and he was rated as one of the tougher nuts of the second echelon of Tour regulars. When he won his second tournament, the Westchester Classic of 1976, Graham finally broke the shackles of his past, buying out the management contract which had bound him to virtual servitude. At last, at the age of 30, he was his own man and free to pursue his destiny without encumbrances, and his only worry concerned the progress of the Dallas Cowboys football team. The emancipation of Graham was reflected in his results, most notably in his victory in the PGA championship of 1979. He had finally reached the lofty plateau of the champions and he thoroughly confirmed his right to that lofty station in golf by winning the US Open championship at Merion two years later. His final round on that occasion was the very model of consistency because he hit every green in regulation figures, golf of a standard which might have been the envy of another Merion winner, the great Ben Hogan himself.

US Open champion 1981. PGA champion 1979. Winner World Cup (with Bruce Devlin) 1970.

Ron Wootton

HAROLD HENNING

b. Johannesburg, South Africa, 3 October, 1934

Great players acquire an aura. Mostly it is self-assurance, sometimes spiked with a hint of arrogance, accompanied by an air of preoccupation and of being in brisk transit to an important engagement. It happens naturally, because if champions pause to smell the flowers along the way, as advocated by Walter Hagen, they are liable to be engulfed by autograph hunters and glad-handers. Harold Henning never took on an aura of any kind. He was never lionised, or featured in magazine profiles or commissioned to contribute instructional hints. That is the way he wanted it, a low profile and a quiet life as one of the boys. Without an aura, Henning failed to gain full recognition of his successes and it is true to say that at no time was he the dominant player on any of the world circuits which he played. As a result his record was likely to be overlooked. Even in his native South Africa his reputation was as the second best of the four Henning brothers, the stay-at-home Allan being considered the superior striker and Brian the most famous, having acquired a considerable aura as tournament director of the South African PGA and later an international reputation in a similar capacity for the American Senior PGA Tour. Yet few players since the war notched up so many victories as Harold Henning, known from Durban to Dallas as Harold the Horse. He spread them about unobtrusively, here a South African Open championship, there a Texas Open, and further afield a Malaysian Open. He had 14 wins in Britain and Europe alone, the last being the 1981 Dutch Open. What was so remarkable about that victory was that it marked his return to competitive play after a seven-year sabbatical during which he played no golf at all. During that lay-off he played a little snooker and generally lived a life of indolence until his wife — and who can blame her? — urged him to snap out of it and get back onto the tournament trail. By then he was approaching his 50th birthday and his brother's Senior Tour, a golfing land flowing with easy dollars, was beginning to beckon. Harold the Horse slipped easily back into tournament harness, sharpening his game on the European circuit in readiness for the golden autumn of his career. The invisible predator of golf was back on the prowl, ready to snatch more juicy morsels from under the noses of the kings of the golfing jungle.

South African Open champion 1957, 1962. South African PGA champion 1965, 1966, 1967, 1972. Member of ten World Cup teams, winning (with Gary Player) in 1965.

Mike Francis

BEN HOGAN

b. Dublin, Texas, 13 August, 1912

That phrase about a man becoming a legend in his own lifetime has become thoroughly worn out in the service of show business hype as an introduction to third rate performers. In the case of Ben Hogan it is no less than prosaic fact and, as is the way with legends, an element of mythology has grown around his career. In the popular myth Hogan never hit a less than perfect shot in his life and if only his putting had matched his striking he would have won every tournament he entered. The truth is rather different and more meritorious. Hogan really had three careers. The slightly built young Texan who joined what was then more of a vagabond golfing circus than a formal tournament circuit at the height of the Depression was a wild over-swinger with a bad grip who could not earn enough money from his golf to survive without taking on part-time jobs. He was 30 years old before he won the first of his 63 professional tournaments. That victory, which marked the start of his second career phase, was the result of a thorough reappraisal of his technique and deep analysis of the mechanics of golf. Then he started to win, at an unprecedented pace and with a style which elevated golf to a new level of performance. That career ended on a foggy morning in early 1949 when he was almost killed in a head-on car crash. The raging competitive fires within him pulled him through but, while he retained his mastery of the swing, his injuries remained a severe handicap for the rest of his golfing life. He won, most notably on one of the most sentimental occasions in golf, the year after his accident in the US Open at Merion, and continued to win, with three of the classic championships in 1953. But he also began to finish second and third in championships which he would never have allowed to elude him at peak fitness. Then his putting, which had never been consistently of championship standard, betrayed him pitilessly. While still able to out-play every rival from tee to green with the most complete mastery of the golf ball ever achieved, he was forced out of competitive play by his total inability to control the putter. So the legend of Ben Hogan really derives from a period of ten years or so, years when he came closer to golfing perfection than any player before or since. The legendary status was thoroughly deserved.

US Open champion 1948, 1950, 1951, 1953. Open champion 1953. Masters champion 1951, 1953. US PGA champion 1946, 1948. Winner (with Sam Snead) Canada Cup (World Cup) 1956.

Rodger Towers

HALE IRWIN

b. Joplin, Missouri, 3 June, 1945

Walter Hagen had a point when he decreed: 'Anybody can get lucky and win the Open once; it takes a real champion to win it twice.' By that standard, and any other, Hale Irwin is a true champion and yet, meeting him on a train and falling into conversation with him, you would never guess that he was a famous athlete and twofold an athlete at that. With his serious mien, erudition and the slightly scholarly look imparted by his spectacles, you might be forgiven for imagining that he was a scientist, possibly something in computers from Silicon Valley. It may be a cliché to say that appearances are deceptive but the virtue of clichés is that they embody truth. Irwin's first sporting distinction was as an outstanding college footballer (University of Colorado), one of those armoured titans of the gridiron and excelling in one of the toughest positions on the field as a defensive back, a human battering ram. Fortunately golf claimed his allegiance and when he joined the PGA Tour in 1968 he quickly demonstrated the truth of the adage that golf is played mostly in the mind. Apart from an exceptional skill with the fairway woods, Irwin's golf was respected as a sound professional method without being outstanding. After all, everyone who makes it onto the Tour is, by definition, a good striker. What set Irwin apart was the intellectual content of his play and an unsuspected steely core to his competitive nature. The other players described him as being smart-tough. That may not be the most elegant of phrases but it well expresses the special qualities which have won Irwin 15 victories in sixteen years of remarkable consistency. In the late seventies he went three years, a span covering 86 tournaments, without missing the halfway cut. All victories count the same in the record books but clearly there are wins and wins, with more merit attaching to those achieved on exceptionally difficult courses. Irwin's record reads like a list of America's greatest courses: Pete Dye's masterpiece, Harbour Town, for the Heritage Classic (twice); Jack Nicklaus's magnum opus, Muirfield Village, for the Memorial tournament; Winged Foot and Inverness GC; Butler National and Atlanta. The plodding journeymen do not win on such courses; it takes a classic golfer to conquer a classic course. Obviously when a great course is used for a great championship the problems are compounded. The preparation of Winged Foot for the 1974 US Open turned the course into a monster, virtually unplayable for the majority of the field. Irwin's smart-tough golf overcame both the course and the occasion, and he qualified under the Walter Hagen definition by repeating that triumph in the US Open of 1979 at Inverness.

US Open champion 1974, 1979. Winner (with John Mahaffey) World Cup, 1979, and individual winner. Member of four Ryder Cup teams.

Rodger Towers

TONY JACKLIN

b. Scunthorpe, Lincolnshire, 7 July, 1944

In the early sixties a wealthy British businessman, Ernest Button, sponsored a scheme under which promising young professionals would be coached and drilled by specialists, in the hope of producing a new British champion. One of the candidates who was auditioned for this sponsorship was Tony Jacklin. The trial took place at Crans-sur-Sierre in Switzerland and Jacklin completed his round by driving the last three holes, all of them par-fours. Mr Button interviewed Jacklin in the club-house afterwards and turned him down, declaring after their meeting: 'That boy will never make a champion'. That opinion was in direct contrast with Jacklin's often expressed insistence that he was going to win the Open. And, of course, that is exactly what he did in 1969 at Royal Lytham and St Annes. The following year Jacklin demoralised the field at Hazeltine, Minnesota, with a runaway victory in the US Open championship, becoming the first Englishman since Harry Vardon to hold the two premier titles simultaneously and the first English winner of the American title since Ted Ray in 1920. By the yardstick of the record books it may seem that Jacklin was never again quite the same force in the Open championship after those twin triumphs, but the truth is that he was dogged by the cruellest luck. His defence of the Open title at St Andrews began with golf of extraordinary virtuosity. He was out in 29 and had a birdie at the tenth when the momentum of his play was broken by a cloudburst which halted play for the day. At Muirfield he was coasting to victory when his playing companion, Lee Trevino, who confessed that he had mentally conceded the victory to Jacklin, chipped in at the 17th and Jacklin was so thrown out of his stride by this cruel fluke that he three-putted. Again at Lytham in 1974 he was going great guns when he took a drop from a rabbit hole and, believing that the ball had rolled into an excessively fortuitous lie, he sportingly re-dropped and was subsequently penalised. Jacklin was a player for whom mood was everything and, once that delicate state of mind had been destroyed, he became just another player. Jacklin continued to win important tournaments and in the early seventies he agreed to abandon his lucrative career on the American Tour in order to provide star quality for the new European circuit. His putting, essentially a function of mood and self-belief, eventually curtailed his competitive appearances, a fate which had overtaken many another world-beater.

Open champion 1969. US Open champion 1970. Member of eight Ryder Cup teams, including non-playing captain 1983.

Mike Francis

DON JANUARY

b. Plainview, Texas, 20 November, 1929

There are golfers and instructors who preach the doctrine that it is impossible to stand too close to the ball at the address. Johnny Miller is an example of a top flight performer who advocates and practises such a style, swinging the club in about as upright a plane as it is humanly possible to achieve. Orthodox teaching suggests that for most people to stand close to the ball at the address is to result in them standing too close to the ball after they have struck it. Don January had an orthodox method as an amateur when he was a stalwart of an all conquering North Texas State university team. He turned pro after serving with the US Air Force and immediately became a winner with a voracious appetite for regular tournament play. His punishing programme induced problems in the region of his lower back and he adopted a markedly upright swing to reduce the strain, at the same time acquiring a lazy tempo to match his slow Texan drawl. That relaxed method was to prove to be one of the most effective and enduring swings in American golf. He was still competing successfully when he turned 50 and qualified for the new Senior Tour and he divided his time between the two circuits, quickly matching his 12 victories on the PGA Tour with a dozen on the Senior Tour, making him the most successful player in its brief history. In three years he finished second, second and first in the money list, with total winnings of nearly half a million dollars. His stroke average that third year was 69.46, suggesting that he was still improving at the age of 54 since the one occasion when he won the Vardon Trophy his average had been 70.32. His big year was 1967 when he beat Don Massengale by two strokes, 69 to 71, in a play-off for the US PGA championship at Columbine country club, near Denver. That qualified him for the Tournament of Champions the following year, which he won, but the evergreen January had an even more memorable success in that tournament in 1976 by beating all the previous year's winners at the age of 46. The quiet Texan earned the abiding respect of his fellow professionals and in 1970 they voted him into the position of player-director of the tournament policy board.

US PGA champion 1967. Member of two Ryder Cup teams.

Mike Francis

TONY LEMA

b. Oakland, California, 25 February, 1934

In the word-association game the name of Tony Lema commonly evokes one of three responses: Champagne, or blowing a seven-stroke lead with 16 to play against Gary Player in the world match-play championship, or winning the Open at St Andrews without ever playing a practice round. All three answers do less than justice to a fine player, inferring as they do that he was a playboy whose dedication to his profession was less than totally professional. Respect for his memory demands that those associations be given a proper perspective. In a light-hearted moment he told the press that he would buy them champagne when he won his first tournament, a tithe he was only too willing to pay after his first two bleak years of campaigning on the American Tour. He was as good as his word and continued the practice after all his victories, thus pioneering a tradition which became a gracious element of professional golf. It is true that Lema enjoyed the good things of life, as might be expected of the son of a penniless Portuguese immigrant who learnt his golf while caddying in San Francisco. He did not make a fetish of practice, flaunting his dedication on tournament ranges, but preferred to hone his game in private, often spending hours hitting shots off the concrete pathway of his manager's home at Winged Foot. The world match-play incident arose from a combination of two factors: Gary Player's wizardry over the closing holes and the fact that Lema had run out of the tablets he was required to take regularly for a heart condition and became increasingly groggy as the day wore on. The ex-marine and Korean war veteran was 30 when he arrived a bare thirty-six hours before the start of the 1964 Open championship at St Andrews, leaving him time for only nine holes of exploration of the Old Course. That seemingly unprofessional approach was in fact a carefully calculated risk. He was playing well, four wins that season, and knew that he was guaranteed thirty years of concentrated experience of the Old Course in the person of Tip Anderson, Arnold Palmer's regular caddie. Anderson tested the wind and advised: Forget the wedge this week and play the small ball. Lema concurred. They made the perfect partnership, based on mutual respect. Anderson called the shots and Lema played them. Leading after 36 holes, Lema said of the course: 'I feel that I have been visiting an old grandmother. She's crochety and eccentric, but also elegant and anyone who doesn't fall in love with her has no imagination.' He won by five strokes, typically gave all the credit to Anderson and sent for champagne. Two years later he and his wife were killed in a plane crash and golf lost more than an elegant striker of the ball.

Open champion 1964. Member of two Ryder Cup teams.

Ivan Rose

GENE LITTLER

b. San Diego, California, 21 July, 1930

The hobby reveals the man. It is impossible to imagine a more appropriate hobby for Gene Littler than his devotion to collecting and restoring vintage Rolls Royces. In the golfing sense he was himself a vintage Rolls Royce; the loudest thing about him was the ticking of his watch. The American press, which has Van Gogh's ear for euphony, tagged him Gene the Machine and Littler had to bear the cross of that nickname for all of his career. Worse, the sports writers began to believe the implications of that label and presented him as a golfing automaton with a swing which simply had to be switched on at the start of a round and it would repeat endlessly on oiled bearings with mechanical precision. Littler explained quietly that not a day passed when he did not have to make an adjustment to his technique, sometimes several small changes in the course of one round. It did not help; he was stuck with his robot image and gave up fighting it. In fact Littler's swing was a model of classic elegance, a true swing rather than the combination swing-hit favoured by the majority of professionals. Littler's method served him well as an amateur, US Amateur champion in 1953, and the following year while still an amateur he rocked the world of pro golf by winning the San Diego Open. That victory earned him nothing but glory, of course, but it proved to be the key to a treasure chest. It meant that he could become a tournament professional without going through any qualifying procedures and, as a winner, he was exempt from the qualifying rounds for all tournaments that year. Indeed, from that day on Littler never had to qualify for a PGA Tour event. Four victories the following season, including the prestige of the Tournament of Champions which he was to defend successfully in the following two years, firmly established Littler as a major figure in golf. The ultimate confirmation of that status came in 1961 at Oakland Hills where he finished strongly, taking over the lead on the 68th hole and resisting all challenges to capture the US Open. Littler missed almost the entire 1972 season because of an operation for cancer of the lymph glands and it was feared that even if he survived this ordeal he would never be able to play golf again. The wiry Littler not only made a full recovery but the following year he won the St Louis Children's Hospital Classic, an emotional triumph which won him the Ben Hogan award, the trophy which recognises courageous golfing revivals after serious illness. Two years later Littler played in his seventh Ryder Cup match after winning three tournaments. He was also the recipient of the Bobby Jones award for outstanding sportsmanship. Golf never had a more fitting nominee for that distinction.

US Open champion 1961. Masters champion of Australia and Japan (twice). 29 PGA tournament victories. 3 Senior Tour victories.

Mike Francis

BOBBY LOCKE

b. Germiston, South Africa, 20 November, 1917

Golfing style, no less than the classic techniques of other sports, is important and rightly forms the basis of formal teaching. However, it is a means to an end, the end being delivery of the club-head at high speed and square to the target line flush to the ball. Contact between club and ball lasts for less than half a millisecond and provided those conditions are fulfilled during that instant in time then the shot will be a good one. No golfer ever exemplified better the truth that the impact position is what matters, regardless of how it is achieved, than Bobby Locke of South Africa. He played from a markedly closed stance and his flat, looping swing imparted an exaggerated but marvellously controlled draw on every shot. His putting stroke, probably the finest ever seen, was a miniature version of his idiosyncratic swing. His greatest assets, however, were an acute golfing brain and a temperament of unshakable placidity. A glittering amateur career was interrupted by the war, which he spent as a bomber pilot of the South African Air Force serving in the Middle East, and afterwards he took the world of golf by storm. He and Peter Thomson dominated the Open championship in the post-war era, with Locke winning the title four times. In the 1957 Open at St Andrews Locke marked his ball one putter-head's length aside, off the line of the putt of his playing companion, inevitably Thomson. In the euphoria of the moment Locke forgot to replace his ball before holing the winning putt and when this error came to light later it presented the championship committee with a dilemma, since Locke had played his ball from a wrong place and was technically liable for a penalty, or even disqualification. However, the chairman of the committee wrote Locke a letter saying that since he had a three-stroke lead a penalty would not affect the outcome and would not be imposed. The result would stand. That letter became Locke's most treasured possession. At the encouragement of Sam Snead, whom he beat twelve times in a series of 16 matches in South Africa, Locke tried his luck in America in 1947, winning six tournaments, finishing second twice and was only once lower than seventh. He was scarcely less successful the following year and his plundering of the tournament coffers generated such hostility among the American professionals that he was forced to confine his unique talents to Britain and South Africa, where he was a popular and welcome champion, among the greatest of all time.

Open champion 1949, 1950, 1952, 1957. South African Open champion nine times. South African Amateur champion 1935, 1937.

Rodger Towers

LLOYD MANGRUM

b. Trenton, Texas, 1 August, 1914

The younger generations may raise an eyebrow at the inclusion of Lloyd Mangrum in a list of the world's greatest golfers. Mangrum? The record books, which are the enduring measure of a golfer, hardly endorse his inclusion. Winner of one US Open championship, a couple of near misses in the classics, a few tournament victories and Ryder Cup appearances. The record books suggest that he was a solid professional but hardly one of the greats, worthy to rub shoulders with Jones and Nicklaus. The record books report facts but they do not convey the truth. Ask Byron Nelson or Ben Hogan. On the tee Mangrum was no more than a workmanlike professional and the same is true up to the vicinity of the green. From then on Mangrum was supreme, one of the game's greatest artists of the touch shots and the putter. He regarded himself as just a working pro, more interested in the purse than fancy titles, and always ready to back himself in a head to head encounter, no matter how illustrious the opponent. The war interrupted his career and may well have distorted his record because he was just getting into his stride as a golfer when he was picked for the 1939 Ryder Cup match. That match was never played and Mangrum had sterner foes to face, in the invasion of Normandy. He was wounded and returned home a hero, but not before he had demonstrated that he had not lost his golfing touch by winning the US Army championship in Paris and the GI championship at St Andrews. In the 1946 US Open championship at Canterbury Mangrum tied with Vic Ghezzi and Byron Nelson. He seemed to be out of his class in the 36-hole play-off but he edged back into contention when he holed a 75-foot putt on the ninth green during the second circuit. Even so he was three strokes behind Ghezzi and two adrift of Nelson with six holes to play. The putter got him home, with three birdies in those last six holes. He was in another play-off for the Open, at Merion in 1950, and on that occasion he literally blew his chance. He was penalised two strokes when he picked up his ball to blow a bug off it. Mangrum was unconcerned, readily conceding that he never read rule books. 'I don't know the traffic regulations of every city I get to either,' he said, 'but I manage to drive through without getting arrested.' Mangrum's real forte was match-play, winning six of his eight Ryder Cup singles. He was selected to captain the American team in 1953 and took part in one of the historic encounters of the series, losing on the 36th hole to one man who could match his uncompromising competitive nature, the redoubtable Eric Brown.

US Open champion 1946. Member of five Ryder Cup teams.

Rodger Towers

GRAHAM MARSH

b. Kalgoorie, Australia, 14 January, 1944

In the companion volume to this book, *The Lord's Taverners Fifty Greatest Cricketers*, Rodney Marsh is acclaimed as Australia's finest wicketkeeper-batsman. Now his elder brother Graham completes a unique family double as an automatic selection as one of the outstanding golfers of the post-war era. 'Swampy', as distinct from 'Irongloves', had no ambitions in professional sport in the early days. He had a career as a school teacher in Perth and golf, as a regular member of the Western Australia team, came second. His dilemma was that in golf he did not come second. He mopped up everything that amateur golf had to offer in the state and when he won the Western Australian Amateur championship and reached the final of the national championship in 1967 he was advised by Peter Thomson, who recognised a rare talent in need of fresh challenges, to try professional golf. Marsh made the transition smoothly and he soon recognised the possibilities for an itinerant tournament specialist. He had to travel immense distances from his home, anyway, even for Australian domestic tournaments, and so he might as well extend his sphere of operations worldwide. It was a plan which could be undertaken only by someone who had the resilience to withstand the strain of constant intercontinental travel and Marsh adopted a lifestyle with a heavy emphasis on regular physical training and physical fitness. Nobody before had attempted to play professional golf as a specialist globe-trotter, thinking nothing of playing on four continents in the space of a month, and he made the system work. The year after he turned pro he won the Singapore Open and followed that success with wins in New Zealand, Switzerland, India, Japan and Britain. Eventually he accepted that his status as an international player would not be fully established until he had proved himself on the American PGA Tour and he gave himself two seasons to prove his point, winning the Heritage Classic in his first year. That year he also confirmed his standing as one of the world's leading players by winning the world match-play championship at Wentworth. Marsh resumed his globetrotting with accelerating success, particularly in south-east Asia and Japan where his sportsmanship and skill made him a folk hero among the country's legion of golf fanatics. Marsh lost track of the exact number of his victories around the world, but at the last official count it was 47.

Ron Wootton

R J WOOTTON

CARY MIDDLECOFF

b. Halls, Tennessee, 6 January, 1921

These days the word amateur has become a pejorative term for a bungled job and the adjective amateurish is positively insulting. The amateur golfer, both in fact and by definition, is someone who does not make too good a thing out of his golf and in many cases the major amateur titles are seen simply as bargaining levers for winning fat professional contracts. Compare that state of affairs with the example of Cary Middlecoff, a crack amateur golfer and US army dentist when he finished his military service after the war. The United States Golf Association invited Middlecoff to join the Walker Cup team in 1947. He felt bound in all honesty to decline, on the grounds that he had a mind to turn professional later. His high integrity and high intelligence were indeed soon working their beneficial influences on the PGA Tour, particularly as a member and then chairman of the tournament committee. His swing was admired for its elegance, although this approval was tempered in some quarters by the deliberation of his play, for the forties were days when three and a half hours was considered dawdling for a round of golf. Middlecoff was one of the new breed of professionals who analysed and annotated every aspect of golf mechanics, sometimes to the detriment of their games. In Middlecoff's case it proved extremely effective. He won the third tournament of his professional career and within two years he was the national champion, winning the 1949 US Open at Medinah with a sandwich performance: two brilliant sub-70 rounds packed between the two bread-and-butter 75s. Seven years later he repeated that triumph with a much more consistent run at Oak Hill, pipping Julius Boros and Ben Hogan by a stroke with 71,70,70,70. If those classics were the cherries on the cake of Middlecoff's career, his best year in strictly professional terms was 1955 when he won six tournaments and was never once outside the top ten. Like many tall men who hit the ball exceptionally hard, and Middlecoff was noted as one of the longest straight drivers of his day, he began to suffer with problems in his back and this infirmity decided him to retire from competitive golf before he had achieved the full promise of his talents. His instructional writing on golf is respected as some of the most authoritative work in this field.

US Open champion 1949, 1956.

Ron Wootton

JOHNNY MILLER

b. San Francisco, California, 29 April, 1947

If ever the gods favoured a young golfer it was surely Johnny Miller. While he was still at Brigham Young University he volunteered to caddie in the US Open championship of 1966 at the Olympic Club, San Francisco. He hoped that he might just possibly get to carry the bag of one of the stars, maybe even Jack Nicklaus's. Such are the dreams of youthful fantasy but they were nothing compared to what actually happened. Just for the hell of it the lanky 19-year-old entered for the qualifying contest and he won a place in the championship field, greatly to his surprise. Greatly to the world's surprise he emerged as a real threat. Instead of carrying Nicklaus's clubs, he was playing alongside the great man and matching him shot for shot, eventually finishing eighth. It was the stuff of juvenile fiction, corny, romantic and implausible, but it happened and when Miller turned pro he was hailed as the new star-in-waiting and wooed by big business seeking the endorsement of this blond Adonis for their products, one contract alone guaranteeing him a million dollars. He had to justify this surge of enthusiasm and quickly made good his early promise. In the final round of the 1973 US Open championship at a waterlogged Oakmont, Miller, starting from well down the field, scored a championship record 63 and had to wait to see if the leaders could match his 279 total. They couldn't and Miller's career went into an even steeper climb. His cool, almost detached temperament and his upright swing brought him victory after victory, often with record scores, culminating in his triumph in the Open championship of 1976 at Royal Birkdale. Then, with the suddenness of a tap being turned off, Miller's golden gusher dried up. He game went sour and he sank into a deep and mysterious slump. He could not explain it and all the advice of professional analysts proved to be of no avail. The most plausible explanation was that this home-loving husband and father recoiled from the upheaval of lionisation which goes with the territory of being a great champion and subconsciously determined that there was more to life than golf. He spent nearly four years in the golfing wilderness before recapturing his winning golf, claiming a regular place in the top twenty of the American Tour after slumping to 111th position.

US Open champion 1973. Open champion 1976. Individual and team winner (with Jack Nicklaus) World Cup 1973. Individual and team winner (with Lou Graham) World Cup 1975. Member of two Ryder Cup teams.

Rodger Towers

KEL NAGLE

b. North Sydney, Australia, 21 December, 1920

He nothing common did or mean
Upon that memorable scene.

Those words might have been written expressly to celebrate Kel Nagle's gracious decoration of the golfing scene. The quiet Australian champion came up the hard way, collecting balls on the practice ground on a course near his Sydney home and then being frozen out of golf by the Australian PGA which put a two year ban on recruits to the profession. The war, during which he served in the jungles of New Guinea, further postponed his golfing ambitions and so he was 29 before his career began to take off with a good win over strong opposition in the 1949 Australian PGA championship. His solid play brought him selection for the Australian Canada Cup (World Cup) team and he formed a devastating partnership with Peter Thomson, winning the trophy in 1954 at Laval-sur-Lac, Montreal and again in 1959 in Melbourne. The following year he confirmed his status as a champion of world class in the centenary Open at St Andrews. Arnold Palmer was the popular favourite, a folk hero of legendary dimensions seeking to add golf's oldest title to his array of honours and, incidentally, giving the Open a much needed lift simply by his first appearance in the tournament. A typical Palmer charge had cut Nagle's four stroke lead to two in the final round and then, to a huge roar, Palmer claimed another birdie on the last hole. Nagle, playing behind, had to play out the last two holes in par to win and the treacherous Road Hole waited with its formidable armoury of defences to claim another victim. Nagle played it as a three-shotter, laying up short with his second and pitching to ten feet. That putt had to go in if Nagle was to prevail and it presented about as severe a test of nerves as golf can offer. Nagle's nerve was equal to the task and he safely negotiated the innocuous 18th for victory by a stroke. Palmer's conquest had to wait until the following year. Five years later Nagle almost pulled off the game's most envied double, victory in the Open championships on both sides of the Atlantic, when he tied with Gary Player at Bellerive for the US Open, losing the play-off by three strokes. The enduring nature of Nagle's simple style was proved in 1971 when he beat Julius Boros for the World Seniors championship.

Open champion 1960. Winner (with Peter Thomson) World
Cup 1954, 1959. Australian Open champion 1959. World
Seniors champion 1971.

Rodger Towers

BYRON NELSON

b. Fort Worth, Texas, 4 February, 1912

A tally of five major championships would be more than enough for any player to be included in a list of the world's great golfers, and near the top at that. By the same token, anyone who won 13 tournaments in one season would be singled out as a phenomenon among tournament professionals. Yet few people today recall those outstanding achievements, even if they are aware of them, when the name of Byron Nelson is mentioned. His indelible claim to fame was his feat, surely the most impregnable record in golf, of winning eleven official PGA tournaments in succession. Nelson was a contemporary and near neighbour of Ben Hogan when they went into tournament golf and in those early days Nelson was incomparably the superior player. He was reaching the height of his extraordinary powers at the outbreak of war, from which he was excluded because of haemophilia, and so was denied the opportunity to compete in many classic championships at a time when he was best equipped to win them. Tournament golf thus was Nelson's war work, and a most valuable contribution it made as a fund-raising activity, with the meagre prize money also being paid in war bonds, and there were plenty of accomplished golfers on hand to offer worthy competition. It was 1944 when Nelson won 13 of the 23 events he played and everyone knew that nobody was ever going to approach such a phenomenal streak again. That opinion failed to convince the tall Texan. The following year he won 18 tournaments, eleven of them in a row. These days, when the world of golf is bombarded with hype about golfing standards ascending unprecedented heights and getting better every week, some young professionals tend to be dismissive of Nelson's results, assuming that the courses he played must have been rinky dink tracks of 5000 yards and, anyway, he had nobody to beat. Well the courses are still there, much as they were in 1945 except that the greens are truer these days, for anyone to challenge Nelson's scoring. His stroke average that year was 68.33, a mark which no-one has beaten before or since. That season took a terrible physical and mental toll from the intense Nelson and he was never a serious force in golf again. Within two years he was in virtual retirement on his ranch in Texas, apart from occasional forays onto the championship scene. He concentrated on teaching golf, for which he earned a considerable reputation among tournament stars, and contributed expert commentaries for television.

*US Open champion 1939. Masters champion 1937, 1942.
US PGA champion 1940, 1945. Member of three Ryder Cup
teams and non-playing captain 1965.*

Ron Wootton

LARRY NELSON

b. Fort Payne, Alabama, 10 September, 1947

None of the golfing stereotypes relates to Larry Nelson. He was not introduced to golf as a caddie; he did not get a grounding in the game in a junior golf programme as a member of the country club set; he did not graduate as a tournament professional via a college golf scholarship; he had no experience of any kind as an amateur golfer. His sports were basketball and baseball at school and his college education at Southern Tech was interrupted when he was called up for two years of military service. Afterwards he took a job as an illustrator with the Lockheed company and he was 22 years old before he first touched a golf club. Even then it was only as an exploratory diversion, hitting balls at a driving range. He enjoyed the experience so much that soon afterwards he took a job in the shop of a local golf professional. That gave him the opportunity to work on his game under expert supervision and after six months he turned professional. He had a fling at some of the minor mini-tour events and in his first full 72-hole tournament, the Florida State Open, he played himself into a good position to win but dropped strokes to par on the last two holes to lose by a stroke. He was sufficiently encouraged to try for his PGA Tour credentials and, despite his lack of experience, gained his card at the first attempt. Nelson was therefore not just a rookie when he joined the Tour, he was a novice and it took him some time to complete his education as a tournament professional. After five years of campaigning he won his first tournament and it was then that he established himself as a major force in professional golf. In the PGA championship of 1981 at the Atlanta Athletic Club he was handed victory by an astonishing series of misadventures and mistakes by his rivals in the leading group. By coincidence there was also an element of freakishness about his second classic victory in the 1983 US Open at Oakmont. Nelson had unobtrusively played himself into contention with successively better rounds of 75, 73, 65 and in the rain delayed final round he faced a 62-foot putt on the green of the par-three 16th hole. His main concern was not to three-putt and he lagged the ball up to the vicinity of the hole, only to see it drop for a birdie, to his astonishment and delight. He won by a stroke over Tom Watson, with his 132 for the last two rounds setting a US Open record. The quiet man of American golf played the golf of his life in the Ryder Cup Match of 1979 at The Greenbrier, gaining maximum points and carrying the US team to victory.

US Open champion 1983. US PGA champion 1981. Member
of two Ryder Cup teams.

Mike Francis

JACK NICKLAUS

b. Columbus, Ohio, 21 January, 1940

To list Jack Nicklaus among the top 50 modern golfers is rather like referring to Shakespeare as being among the dramatists of sixteenth-century Stratford-on-Avon. Jack Nicklaus *is* modern golf. By the age of 25 he had won every major honour in the game. So he won them all over again, and again, until he had amassed 19 of the major championships, 69 American PGA tournaments, 18 international titles, six World Cup victories, honours in six Ryder Cup teams and successful captaincy of a seventh. The records go on and on, towering above the achievements of any other player in the history of golf and setting a standard which will surely never be surpassed. The records are eloquent testimony to the quality of his golf and, by natural extension, to the quality of the man but they tell nothing of the important subject of the style of Jack Nicklaus. His contribution to golf as a remarkable person may well be even greater than that impregnable roll of honours as a player. When Nicklaus turned pro as a burly, crew-cut winner of two US Amateur championships, and unquestionably destined to become the dominant figure in world golf, Arnold Palmer was at the height of his popularity, the hero of the nation. Here was this young interloper threatening a national institution and Nicklaus's career was launched against a flood tide of abuse and hostility. Never once did he respond to the boos and catcalls and insults, either by spoken protest or gesture. Here, clearly, was more than a great player. Here was an exceptional man and an outstanding sportsman. Golf could not have had a better exemplar. Nicklaus changed the direction of professional golf by his approach to tournament play. He analysed courses with intense thoroughness, a habit which was to stand him in good stead when he later turned his talents to course designing, and carefully plotted the approach angles which minimised the dangers and maximised his scoring potential. He pioneered the practice of personally pacing yardages for the approach shots. He estimated winning totals and planned his tactics accordingly. Nobody has ever approached invincibility in golf, because the human factor must always dominate, but by eliminating the element of chance as far as possible through his analytical planning he elevated himself head and shoulders above his rivals. One further factor has contributed hugely to his unique success. Nobody, not even Ben Hogan, has brought a more steadfast concentration and inflexible will to the game of golf and these are the qualities which have earned him his well-deserved reputation as the finest pressure putter in golf. In short, when he is at his best there are two categories of tournament professional: Jack Nicklaus and the rest.

Open champion 1966, 1970, 1978. US Open champion 1962, 1967, 1972, 1980. Masters champion 1963, 1965, 1966, 1972, 1975. US PGA champion 1963, 1971, 1973, 1975, 1980. US Amateur champion 1959, 1961.

Mike Francis

GREG NORMAN

b. Mount Isa, Australia, 10 February, 1955

Most people can look back and reflect on events which appeared insignificant at the time but which proved to be turning points in their lives. For Greg Norman such a moment came when he was in the recruiting office of the Royal Australian Air Force with his father, his hand poised above the enrolment form which would commit him as a trainee fighter pilot and fulfil his boyhood dreams. Norman paused, threw down the pen and announced: 'I'm sorry, but I am going to be a pro golfer.' In the light of his previous experience it was a surprising decision because as a boy Norman had excelled at every sport except golf, which he considered to be a cissy pursuit. It was only because he had allowed himself to be pressed into service to caddie for his mother that he came into close contact with golf at all. He thought it looked easy, and idly hit some shots on the practice ground after his mother's round. He soon recognised that there was more to golf than patting a ball along. The tall and powerful lad was hooked and channelled all his energies into mastering the frustrating business of controlling a golf ball. His progress was rapid. Within a year of turning pro he won his first tournament in Australia and set off for Britain the next year to learn his trade as a tournament player. He saw this period as a training exercise, refusing to set goals for himself before he had learnt how to compete and how to win. He would not contemplate transferring his allegiance to the American Tour until he had passed his self-imposed graduation test. In retrospect he had reason to feel that he had been ultra cautious, ultra thorough, in persevering with this apprenticeship. He won 14 international tournaments before trying his luck in America, immediately finishing in a tie for the Bay Hill Classic. The following year he consolidated his standing on the American Tour while winning six international events, including his second world match-play championship. In 1984, having established himself with a home in America, he won the Kemper Open, the Canadian Open and tied for first place in most dramatic style in the US Open championship at Winged Foot. He gave everything in that final round and was thoroughly jaded when he played off with Fuzzy Zoeller next day, but the tall Australian had served notice that he had matured into a golfer of the highest class.

Australian Open champion 1980.

Ivan Rose

CHRISTY O'CONNOR

b. Galway, Ireland, 21 December, 1924

It took a lot to upset the affable Christy O'Connor but there was one sure way of putting a steely glint into his eye: Congratulate him on his good fortune of having been blessed with a God-given natural golf swing. Many people made this mistake after watching the fluent style of the powerful Irishman who perhaps came closer than any golfer of his era to mastering the precept that the secret of golf is to hit the ball with your practice swing. On being called a 'natural', O'Connor would growl that behind every shot he hit in public competition lay a grounding of thousands of rehearsals in private practice sessions. As a young assistant he spent months on the beach at Bundoran, hitting shots off the hard sand in all weathers. He said later of this hard apprenticeship: 'There weren't enough hours in the day for me. I was out there morning, noon and night hitting balls until I could hardly stand.' When he felt that he could control the ball in the fiercest gales he moved on to the next stage of his education as a golfer, restricting his tournament play to Ireland for four years. Then he was ready to face anyone. On his first trip across the Irish Sea in 1954, he took Henry Cotton to the 23rd hole in the semi-finals of the Penfold tournament and it was clear that a major new talent had arrived. From then on he was in the forefront of the emerging British professional circuit, claiming the first four-figure cheque and then, in due course, the first five-figure prize. He became an automatic selection for the Ryder Cup team, appearing a record ten times between 1955 and 1973, and an equally permanent fixture in the Irish team for the World (Canada) Cup. In 1958 he was teamed with Harry Bradshaw for the Cup match and, despite the rarified atmosphere of Mexico City and the unfamiliar conditions, they brought the trophy home to Ireland. In 1958 he finished one stroke behind Peter Thomson in the Open championship at Royal Lytham and St Annes, and when he turned fifty his successive victories in the PGA Seniors championship were regarded almost as formalities. Rheumatics in the shoulder eventually forced O'Connor to slow down, although he continued to be a dominant force in Irish golf while devoting most of his time to his club appointment at Royal Dublin.

Member of ten Ryder Cup teams. Member of fifteen Canada and World Cup teams. Winner (with Harry Bradshaw) 1958.

Rodger Towers

ARNOLD PALMER

b. Latrobe, Pennsylvania, 10 September, 1929

While most of the selections for this list of great golfers received unanimous acclaim from the panel, it has to be said that Arnold Palmer was chosen on a split decision. He felt that it was inappropriate for a selector to be included in the list. That opinion was typical of the staunchest defender of the game's proprieties but it was also absurd. The book would have had to be called something like The Fifty Greatest Golfers Not Counting Arnold Palmer, which would have been an affront to logic, not to mention an even greater abuse of the English language. In terms of golf as a major spectator sport, and as a major participant sport, Palmer's contribution was by far the greatest individual influence. Virtually single-handed he took professional golf into the big time. The arrival of Palmer on the professional scene coincided with the expansion of television as a mass medium. The chemistry was perfect. Palmer embodied all the virtues of Western mythology: looks, build, magnetic personality and moral rectitude. Central Casting could not have come up with a more archetypical hero figure, a sporting John Wayne of the middleweight division. Above all, he was human. He played golf like the club members, hitting the ball with all his might and landing in all manner of trouble. But Palmer could recover in miraculous fashion and so the viewers, while they could relate to him, also had to marvel at him. Win or lose, and he did both in exciting style, he was the popular hero. While other golfers were associated with severe Victorian virtues such as dedication, patience and industry, Palmer inspired additions to golf's vocabulary: 'Charge' and 'Charisma' and 'Crisis'. The man and his deeds were drawn on an heroic scale and a generation of Americans was inspired to take up what had been a minority sport for the privileged few. Still more became addicted golf watchers, 'Arnie's Army', and the game and everyone associated with it prospered because of Palmer. Of course, Palmer had no thought of being a crusader in the early days; his simple ambition was to make his way in a game which had been part of his life since childhood, as the son of a hard-working greenkeeper-pro in Pennsylvania. He achieved pretty well every goal the game had to offer but his successes were of less significance than the manner of his play and deportment. Having virtually invented golf as a major sport, he set the standards of sportsmanship and behaviour which were to guide the conduct of his profession.

Open champion 1961, 1962. US Open champion 1960. Masters champion 1958, 1960, 1962, 1964. US Amateur champion 1954. Member of six Ryder Cup teams, non-playing captain 1975. Member of six winning World Cup teams, individual winner 1967.

Mike Francis

JERRY PATE

b. Macon, Georgia, 16 September, 1953

The history of golf is embellished with individual shots of exceptional brilliance or significance, such as Gene Sarazen's four-wood into the hole at Augusta's long fifteenth for an albatross and the foundations of his Masters victory in 1935, Bobby Jones's mashie shot into the seventeenth green at Lytham for his first Open championship victory in 1926, Arnold Palmer's recovery from the willow scrub at Royal Birkdale on the way to winning the 1961 Open. Jerry Pate will long be associated with two such strokes of brilliance, both with the five-iron. As a rookie on the American Tour, Pate was a rather surprising contender for the US Open championship of 1976 at the Atlanta Athletic Club when he took an ultra cautious line across the lake at the last hole and sent his ball into the tangle of ankle-high rough across the fairway. By lucky chance it finished in the one spot which had not responded fully to the devoted attention of the USGA to make the rough escape-proof, although the lie was far from propitious. Pate's five-iron shot stopped two feet from the hole and so the tall, former US Amateur champion started his winning career as a pro with the big one. In the 1982 Tournament Players' Championship, the first occasion that the tournament was played on Pete Dye's nightmarish masterpiece, Pate forged through the field with three birdies in the last seven holes, including one on the treacherous island 17th, and thus needed par at the last to get into a play-off. At the 18th, a hole of similar conformation to the 18th at Atlanta, he again hit a five-iron shot to two feet for a winning birdie. True to a personal tradition he had established in winning the Memphis Classic the previous year, he celebrated by diving into the lake, having first expressed the will of his fellow professionals by pushing Pete Dye and Commissioner Deane Beman into the crocodile infested waters. With two classic victories under his belt, plus representative honours in both Walker and Ryder Cup teams, and a solid nucleus of PGA tournament victories, it seemed that this elegant swinger was destined to progress naturally to greater glories. Maybe he would but a pulled muscle in the neck proved intractable, severely hampering the action of a markedly left-sided player. Having never finished outside the top thirty in the American rankings, and gracing the top ten five times in eight years, he fell down the list to 136th in 1983. The injury failed to respond to treatment during 1984 and it was even feared that he might have to abandon his glittering career.

US Open champion 1976. US Amateur champion 1974.
Member of one Walker Cup team and one Ryder Cup team.

Ivan Rose

GARY PLAYER

b. Johannesburg, South Africa, 1 November, 1935

The Rules of Golf restrict every player to 14 clubs. Anyone who has played Gary Player, or has seen him play, is entitled to believe that he has a fifteenth club in his bag, a wondrous implement of the most unyielding steel which enables him to recover from the most unlikely places, to hole long putts at the telling moment and to snatch championships from six, seven, even eight strokes behind the leader. In a way he has. In prosaic terms it is called will power. He started with all the disadvantages of being small, 5′ 7″, of modest physique, and poor. All he had in his favour was fanaticism. He became a food and fitness fanatic, building himself up with a regime of exercises which would have put a champion boxer to shame. He became a highly trained athlete because he had to compete against players nearly twice his size (his own waist exactly matched the thigh measurement of his rival, Jack Nicklaus). He became a golf fanatic, filling every spare moment of the day with practice and experiment. He never acquired a classical swing, being troubled all his career with recurrent faults, and often swung himself off balance, but by sheer industry he trained his hands to deliver the club-head flush to the ball, no matter how unpropitious the swing or the balance. That was enough, in combination with his indomitable fighting spirit, to make him the match, and often the master, of the best golfers in the world. After four years of hard grafting in Britain and South Africa, Player had acquired the cash and the confidence to assault the American PGA Tour. It was hard going for a couple of years but by the end of the fifties he was established and his career soared like an arrow, as he always knew it would. He joined the very select band of golfers who have captured all four of the classic titles of golf, won the world match-play championship no fewer than five times and accumulated 127 major victories around the world, including his own national championship 13 times and the Australian Open championship seven times. What is more he achieved all that as a peripatetic golfer who always retained his home base in South Africa, where he has pursued a separate and barely less successful career as a breeder of thoroughbred horses. As he approached 50 he looked forward to continuing his travels by competing on the Senior Tour, with fresh fields to conquer.

Open champion 1959, 1968, 1974. US Open champion 1965. Masters champion 1961, 1974, 1978. US PGA champion 1962. South African Open champion 13 times. World match-play champion five times. Individual winner World Cup twice.

Ron Wootton

R J WOOTTON

DAI REES

b. Barry, Wales, 31 March, 1913

Confidence is the key to the character of enduring sportsmen, and Dai Rees was never short of self-belief, but the most dominant trait of the ebullient and combative little Welshman was enthusiasm. His relish for life was insatiable and he was blessed with a constitution which enabled him to indulge every passing passion. He trained with the Arsenal football team, often, it seemed, to acquire the stamina to sustain his strength as their most loyal fan and most argumentative protagonist. But mostly, of course, his enthusiasm was for the game of golf, which he started to play at the age of two and went on playing with undiminished zest for the rest of his life. His victories spanned forty years and his massive contributions to the game as an administrator, teacher, lecturer and evangelist continued until the day he died. Rees was the son of a greenkeeper-professional and he could not wait to finish school and begin his own career. He was an assistant when he won his first tournament, the British match-play championship, and that victory won him a place in his first Ryder Cup team. His fighting nature made him an exceptional match-player and his fierce patriotism also inspired him to play better for his country than he did for personal gain. He played in nine Ryder Cup matches between 1937 and 1961, being captain four times and non-playing captain again in 1967. His greatest triumph in the match was at Lindrick in 1957 when his infectious enthusiasm inspired his team to rally after a disastrous foursomes series to win the trophy, he himself leading by example with a decisive 7 and 6 win over Ed Furgol. Rees made up for his short stature with a long swing which he controlled with the unorthodox two-handed, or baseball, grip. He was a regular tournament winner, specially in the match-play championship which he captured four times, but the title which he sought above all, that of Open champion, always eluded him. Normally his score of 286 over Carnoustie might have been good enough but 1953 was the year of the irresistible Ben Hogan, and Rees finished joint second. The following year at Royal Birkdale he again had to play second fiddle to a brilliant talent, that of Peter Thomson at the start of his dominating championship run. At Birkdale in 1961 Rees alone maintained a challenge to the charging Arnold Palmer, failing by a stroke to force a play-off.

Member of ten Ryder Cup teams, four as playing captain and one as non-playing captain.

Ron Wootton

DOUG SANDERS

b. Cedartown, Georgia, 24 July, 1933

Every tournament professional has to furnish his PGA with formal biographical details for promotional purposes and one of the standard entries on the questionnaire is headed 'Hobbies'. His friends may have looked askance at the answers supplied by Doug Sanders, who listed his hobbies as jogging, fishing and travel. Jogging? Well there was a time when the handsome Sanders may have had to break into a canter to evade jealous husbands and 'Travel', on the evidence of his lurid autobiography, may have covered the more serious contingencies. As for 'Fishing', he was certainly adept at hooking superfluous ice cubes from his glass. Sanders studiously cultivated his public image as a hell-raising playboy and also, with his spectacular golf outfits, as the Beau Brummel of the world's golf circuits. However, beneath the devil-may-care appearances, was an acute golfing brain which he exercised through the most idiosyncratic swing in modern golf. It was said that Sanders learnt to play golf in a phone box but while that crack may have found its essential grain of truth in his short backswing, with the hands never getting past waist height, the exaggerated width of his stance could never have been accommodated in a telephone booth. The real origins of this individual style were the narrow fairways of the Cedartown club, Georgia, where he learnt his golf, in combination with a pressing economic necessity not to lose golf balls. He certainly made the method work, although it imposed undue strains and he had to undergo surgery on his hand and shoulder. He came to prominence at the age of 23 when, still an amateur, he won the Canadian Open championship. He turned pro that same year, 1956, and over the next eighteen years on the PGA Tour he won 20 tournaments. In the classics he was fated to become a specialist runner-up. He was second in the 1959 US PGA championship (and twice third). He was second in the 1961 US Open championship. He was second in the 1966 Open championship, behind Jack Nicklaus, and it was Nicklaus who thwarted him again in 1970. Maybe it would be more accurate to say that Sanders thwarted himself because he needed a 4 on the last hole at St Andrews, pitched strong, putted short and then missed from less than a yard to enable Nicklaus to tie on 283. Nicklaus won the play-off by a stroke. So four strokes denied him four major championships.

Member of the Ryder Cup team 1967.

Rodger Towers

SAM SNEAD

b. Hot Springs, Virginia, 27 May, 1912

Even the fertile imagination of an author of juvenile fiction would be strained to match the story of Sam Snead. A feckless barefoot boy in the backwoods of West Virginia whittles himself a golf club from the branch of a swamp maple tree, swings with such natural grace that he astonishes the golfing community by the unprecedented length of his drives, wins so many tournaments that even the official statisticians of the game cannot keep track of his triumphs, and amasses a huge fortune which, in true hill-billy tradition, he keeps buried in tomato cans on his farm. No, no. Mark Twain would have rejected such a plot as too far-fetched. Well, apart from the tomato cans, a subject which Snead preferred to leave open for speculation among his cronies, it is all well documented fact and that is not the half of it. The tall and lissom boy progressed from caddie to a player of such skill that he was offered an appointment as an assistant professional. Almost immediately he faced dismissal. An influential club member was playing in the group ahead of Snead and a ball pitched among them, too close for comfort. The member made an official complaint that Snead had hit his second shot before the players ahead were out of range and demanded that the youth be fired for his breach of etiquette. Snead went to apologise to the aggrieved member and said that he had surprised himself by the length of that drive. Your *drive?* asked the incredulous member. It could not have been a drive. Nobody could hit a ball that far. But, of course, there were witnesses and the astonished member immediately offered to sponsor Snead in a career of tournament golf. Millions of fans were to be no less astonished by Snead's golf during the following half century. The PGA credits him with 84 official Tour victories. Independent recorders have documented 135 wins. Snead himself believed the figure to be nearer 165, including regional tournaments. The one major honour which eluded him was the US Open championship title but for the rest his story is one of enduring records. He is a member of golf's most select club, of players who have broken 60 on a long and difficult par-72 golf course. For years his annual stroke average was below 70, proof of his remarkable consistency, and his average of 69.23 in 1950 remains the record for the PGA Tour. He is both first and second in the records for the most victories in the same event, having won the Greater Greensboro Open eight times and the Miami Open six. When he won the Greensboro Open for the eighth time in 1965 at the age of 53 he became the oldest winner in the history of the Tour. The catalogue of records and honours went on, just as Snead went on and on. His swing, the very model of leisurely rhythm and flowing grace, brought him fresh records on the Senior Tour. In 1979 he scored his age, 68, in the Quad Cities Open and then improved it with rounds of 67, 66. As a septuagenarian he broke his age so regularly that the feat lost its novelty and was almost expected of him.

Open champion 1946. Masters champion 1949, 1952, 1954.
US PGA champion 1942, 1949, 1951. PGA Senior champion
six times. World Seniors champion five times.

Ivan Rose

PETER THOMSON

b. Melbourne, Australia, 23 August, 1929

Sir Walter Simpson, the nineteenth-century golf historian and essayist, wrote*: 'Excessive golfing dwarfs the intellect. And is this to be wondered at when we consider that the more fatuously vacant the mind is, the better for play? It has long been observed that absolute idiots, ignorant whether they are playing two more or one off two, play steadiest. An uphill game does not make them press, nor victory within their grasp render them careless. Alas! We cannot all be idiots. Next to the idiotic, the dull, unimaginative mind is the best for golf. In a professional competition I would prefer to back the sallow, dull-eyed fellow with a "quid" in his cheek, rather than any eager-looking champion.' Sir Walter never met Peter Thomson. If he had he might have tempered his remarks because there was never a more intellectual golfer than the eager-looking Australian. We might concede half a point to Sir Walter in that, while Thomson was undoubtedly the finest golfer in the world of his era, he might have achieved even greater international triumphs if he had pursued the bitch goddess of success with dull-eyed, single-minded perseverance. That was never Thomson's style. To him golf was always a game, a serious part of life in the right place at the right time, but never the main objective in life. He never chased after the prestige titles of golf with the obsessive zeal of a lepidopterist netting butterflies to add to his collection. Golfing immortality was all very well, but not at the expense of mortality. Thomson's interests ranged from music and writing to course designing and politics. In his prime he played little in the United States, thereby earning the reputation of being anti-American. The slur was never justified; the truth was that he disapproved of the larger American golf ball and preferred the challenge of what he considered to be the more difficult small ball in use in Britain and Australia. When the large ball was universally adopted by professional golf Thomson proved what a force he might have been in America by campaigning with great success on the Senior Tour. Even with his limited programme, Thomson became the dominant player of his time, winning five Open championships in twelve years, a record surpassed only by Harry Vardon.

Open champion 1954, 1955, 1956, 1958, 1965. Won World Cup (with Kel Nagle) 1954, 1959. Champion of Australia (three times) and winner of 16 other national championships.

*The Art of Golf (David Douglas), 1892

Ivan Rose

LEE TREVINO

b. Dallas, Texas, 1 December, 1939

For hundreds of years the caddie shack was the academy from which underprivileged students graduated as professional golfers. Changing social patterns eliminated the caddie shack and Lee Trevino was one of the last, and the most celebrated, alumni of that hard school. Fate dealt the infant Trevino about as unpromising a hand to play as could be imagined. A Mexican-American born into a world of racial bigotry, in the poorest of Texan environments on the wrong side of the tracks, never knowing his father and without the physical assets to fight his way out of the rural slums. His only ace was an acute mind which became sharpened by the daily struggle for existence. Odd jobs at a par-three course introduced him to golf and necessity, in the form of matches in which he played for a dollar with only a nickel in his pocket, proved an unconventional but effective teacher. Trevino learnt, above all, the paramount lesson that getting the ball into the hole in the fewest number of strokes, regardless of style, was the name of this game. Most of that education was directed into his hands and the ability to contrive killing shots from unlikely situations. After a stint in the Marine Corps he took his self-taught game onto the pro circuit but made little impact, mainly because he did not believe in his right to be playing with the mighty stars. He was about ready to call it a day when his wife pawned everything she had to pay his entry for the 1967 US Open. That gave him the stimulus to assert himself and he finished fifth. From that moment his career took off in spectacular fashion and success enabled his ebullient personality to blossom. In 1971 he won the Canadian, British and United States Open championships within the space of a month and was acclaimed as the greatest player in the world. Not even serious injury from being struck by lightning could keep him down, nor a series of business misadventures which dissipated two fortunes. Every time Trevino has bounced back, enslaving the galleries with his wisecracks and his consummate artistry as a shot-maker. Behind the happy-go-lucky clowning lies a ruthlessly serious competitor with the priceless asset of being able to switch off the levity and focus his concentration with fierce intensity as he plays each shot.

US Open champion 1968, 1971. Open champion 1971, 1972. US PGA champion 1984. Member of six Ryder Cup teams, five World Cup teams.

Ron Wootton

ROBERTO DE VICENZO

b. Buenos Aires, Argentina, 14 April, 1923

The axiom that nice guys come second was thoroughly exploded, or possibly proved by the exception, in the case of Roberto de Vicenzo. Nobody finished first more often in the history of golf, with more than 230 victories around the world, and no golfer was more universally popular than the burly Argentinian. The quality of his golf was endorsed by his unprecedented record but there was another measure of his exceptional skill available by simple examination of his clubs. The grooved faces of his irons were smooth over an area the size of a shirt button, precisely on the sweet spot, worn down by his industrious practice sessions and physical proof of the most accurate strike in modern golf. Rudyard Kipling decrees that if you can face triumph and disaster and treat those twin imposters both the same then you are a man, my son. By that standard de Vicenzo was a giant of a man because he confronted the greatest triumph and the most devastating disaster which the game of golf can provide. In 1967 he won the Open championship after many years of trying, holding off the inevitable challenge of Jack Nicklaus over the Royal Liverpool course to capture the title with a score of 278. Less than a year later he trudged through an avenue of delirious fans up to the 18th fairway of the Augusta National golf club, the cheers acknowledging a stupendous round of golf which must tie him with Bob Goalby and force a play-off for the Masters title. De Vicenzo holed out and quickly signed his card. The speed with which he completed this formality had nothing to do with the euphoria of the moment or his happy-go-lucky nature, because he was a thorough professional, but he was distracted by a frenzied TV executive badgering him to come immediately for a quick interview. De Vicenzo's command of English was tenuous and he was confused, believing that he was being summoned to conform with an obligatory element of the Masters tradition. Naturally, he signed his card and obliged. Twenty minutes later the bombshell exploded. De Vicenzo's playing companion and marker, Tommy Aaron, had marked one hole for a 4 instead of the birdie 3 which had been observed by 25,000 spectators and some 14 million television viewers. The officials consulted Bobby Jones himself in their frantic attempts to avoid a grotesque miscarriage of natural justice but the rule was adamant and inflexible: if a player signs for a score higher than the number of strokes he had actually taken then that higher score must stand. Goalby was thus the outright winner, de Vicenzo second. De Vicenzo's reaction was a reprise of his response when he holed the winning putt at Hoylake, a self-deprecating grin and a shrug of the shoulders.

Open champion 1967. Represented Argentina 17 times in World Cup, winning team title with Antonio Cerda in 1953 and individual title in 1969 and 1972.

Ron Wootton

LANNY WADKINS

b. Richmond, Virginia, 5 December, 1949

Every golfer has his ups and downs, commonly thought to be caused by biorhythms, and when he is on an 'up' he is often said to be on a streak. The word should really be reserved for a phenomenon much rarer than a cyclical improvement in form. A genuine streak is an aberration of golfing excellence which may last for several weeks, months even, during which the golfer for no rational reason plays well above his usual form. There was never a more dramatic example of a streak golfer than Lanny Wadkins. Week in and week out he is a solid professional with a distinctive style, hands held very low at the address, the right hand well over the top of the shaft in an exaggeratedly 'weak' position, and with a swing which is considerably faster than the average or, for that matter, the prescribed text-book tempo. The other element in his golf which sets him apart from the general run of modern tournament professionals is that he does not strive to perfect a repeating, standard shot but every time he addresses the ball he seeks to shape his shot, imparting spin to fly the ball high or low, left or right, according to his assessment of the situation. He is thus one of a vanishing breed of players who prefers to work the ball with his hands. Every now and then, for no reason that he can detect, Wadkins enjoys spells when the game is easy. Everything he tries comes off and he enjoys such mastery over the golf ball that he can land it on the fairway or green with as much precision as if he had walked forward and placed it there. At such times his confidence naturally runs high and as a result his putting matches his stroke-making. When Wadkins is on a streak the others are playing for place money and they know it. Of course it is a matter of chance whether these streaks coincide with major or minor events. For instance, he enjoyed a spell of irresistible virtuosity in 1982 which was rather wasted on the Phoenix Open, the Tournament of Champions and the Buick Open when it would have done him so much more good in the great classics. But his golf during these streak periods is sublime and by the law of averages he has had to have spells of top form for the big ones, notably in winning his national Amateur championship, the PGA championship and in some of his Ryder Cup matches. Both as an amateur and as a professional Wadkins has earned a reputation of being the best when he is at his best.

US Amateur champion 1970. US PGA champion 1977.
Member of two Walker Cup teams, three Ryder Cup teams
and one World Cup team.

Ron Wootton

Ronald J. Wigotton

ART WALL

b. Honesdale, Pennsylvania, 25 November, 1923

Not the least of the advantages which golf enjoys over other sports is that it is a game for life. Given a simple method and good health a player can go on enjoying his golf for as long as he likes, and examples of octogenarians beating their age with their score is so commonplace that the successful exponent of this feat is lucky if anybody in the bar is impressed enough to buy him a drink. Art Wall turned pro in 1949 after graduating from Duke University and his career on the PGA Tour went on and on for nearly thirty years. His tally of 14 victories spanned twenty-two years and he also enjoyed exceptional success on the old Caribbean Tour, with another ten victories. An arthritic shoulder eventually curtailed his tournament play but he moved home to Sonoita near the Mexican border and the hot, dry climate worked wonders. The indomitable Wall was back on the tournament trail again as a senior, winning the American National Senior Open in 1978 and following that triumph with two victories on the new PGA Senior Tour. Even if you add his 42 holes in one, graphic evidence of the accuracy of his iron play, and the quality of his golf when in his 52nd year he won the Milwaukee Open with scores of 67, 67, 67, 70 for a total of 17 under par, you might be tempted to classify him as a first-class professional but just short of greatness. It was the season of 1959 that stamped Wall as one of the greats of golf. His big year started with the Masters, although few people suspected that he would be a factor in the tournament when he started the final round six strokes behind Arnold Palmer and Stan Leonard. He had three birdies in the first twelve holes but even then he was only one under par for the day and not offering any severe threat to the leaders. Then Wall went into action, with five birdies over the last six holes for a 66 which gave him victory by a stroke over Cary Middlecoff, with Palmer relegated into third place. Wall went on to win three more tournaments that year, topping the money list, being voted Player of the Year and winning the Vardon Trophy for the season's lowest stroke average of 70.35. Inevitably he was selected for the Ryder Cup team, an important match for the United States that year because the Americans had relinquished the trophy to the British Isles team in 1957. Wall played a large part in avenging that reverse by annihilating Christy O'Connor by 7 and 6 at Palm Desert.

Masters champion 1959. Member of three Ryder Cup teams.

Mike Francis

HARVIE WARD

b. Tarboro, North Carolina, 8 December, 1925

'If the law supposes that,' said Mr Bumble ... 'the law is a ass – a idiot.' 'The first thing we do, let's kill all the lawyers.' Oddly enough, neither Charles Dickens nor William Shakespeare ever had any dealings with golf's laws of amateur status, otherwise they might have put even stronger sentiments into the mouths of their characters. Harvie Ward had good cause to rue the absurdities of the law because they thwarted what many good judges of golf felt to have been the most promising chance of a golfer conquering the worlds of both amateur and professional golf since the days of Bobby Jones. As a young man Ward was a superb player, the best amateur that Arnold Palmer ever saw, and he had good reason for that opinion because Ward was one of the very few men who beat him in his amateur days. That was in the North and South Amateur championship when Ward was still a student at the University of North Carolina, in a field which also included Julius Boros, Frank Stranahan, Doug Ford and Dick Meyer, all destined to become luminaries of professional golf. Victory in that company set Ward on his way and three years later he won the Amateur championship at Prestwick, beating Joe Carr in the semi-final and annihilating Stranahan by 7 and 5 in the final. He took the United States Amateur championship in 1955 and successfully defended his title the following year. He never had a chance to make it three in a row. At that time he was employed by a San Francisco car dealer, Eddie Lowery, who at the age of ten had caddied for Francis Ouimet in his historic victory over Harry Vardon and Ted Ray in the 1913 US Open at Brookline. Lowery was also a member of the United States Golf Association's executive committee by this time, which added to the sensitivity when he was accused of paying expenses to finance Ward's amateur golf. The affair hinged more on book-keeping than morality, since any money paid as salary or commission to Ward would have been entirely legitimate. The USGA decided to make an example of its champion and suspended his amateur status. Ward's golf never regained its glorious flair after that. He lived under a cloud that ought to have been blown away by gales of public ridicule and common sense. Ward's selection for the Walker Cup match of 1959 may be seen as an act of contrition by the USGA or, at least, forgiveness but it was too late to revive that rare talent. Ward turned professional late in life and competed on the Senior Tour.

Amateur champion 1952. US Amateur champion 1955, 1956. Member of three Walker Cup teams.

Rodger Towers

TOM WATSON

b. Kansas City, 4 September, 1949

Tom Watson is often cited as typical of the new generation of professional golfers: stamped out on the production line of the university golf team system and emerging as a ready-made star, needing only the addition of a PGA card to send him purring smoothly along the road to glory. In fact, even if we swallow that dubious analogy of mass production golfers, Watson was never a product of such a process. If the factory metaphor must be pursued he was more of a one-off model, and built by craftsmen and, like most high performance machines, in constant need of fine tuning. For a start he never had a golf scholarship. He went to a genuine seat of learning (Stanford) and earned a genuine degree (Psychology) and when he did turn pro he spluttered and blew up in tournament after tournament. The press dubbed him Huckleberry Finn, presumably on the grounds that he bore a passing resemblance to the description of Tom Sawyer, and wrote him off as chicken. Chicken! How those writers must choke on the bones of their analogies. In many ways Watson is the antithesis of the American tournament professional. He reveres links golf and is upset when an untimely cloudburst or excessive artificial watering removes the built-in bad luck of bump-and-bounce golf. He cares little for glory and less for money, being drawn single-mindedly towards his unattainable goal of golfing perfection. He abhors the limelight and lionisation, jealously preserves his privacy, rules his life according to inflexible liberal principles and, incidentally, plays the guitar to the standard of a professional musician. He also plays golf which, at its best, is in a plane above that of his contemporaries. When Watson learnt the art of winning, something quite separate from the craft of striking a golf ball, he showed his true qualities of resourcefulness and a boldness bordering on recklessness. His finest hour was at the Open championship at Turnberry in 1977 when he was drawn to play with Jack Nicklaus. These two played what may have been the best and second best four rounds of golf ever witnessed, and surely the greatest head to head 'match', and Watson, who had never once been in the lead for 70 holes, prevailed by a single stroke on the last green. The king was dead, long live the king! Watson is not the most consistent of champions but he rises to the great occasions, particularly when facing the challenge of a British championship links. In 1983 he became only the third player in history to be champion golfer five times, equalling Peter Thomson's record and narrowly failing the following year to match Harry Vardon's six championship titles, an honour which was surely postponed rather than denied.

Open champion 1975, 1977, 1980, 1982, 1983. US Open 1982. Masters champion 1977, 1981. Member of three Ryder Cup teams.

Rodger Towers

TOM WEISKOPF

b. Massillon, Ohio, 9 November, 1942

Tom Weiskopf was probably the most misunderstood player in America and the reason for that could very well be that he did not understand himself. He was certainly often at odds with his own perfectionist nature and that gave rise to the impression of a master craftsman who carried within him the seeds of self-destruction. His close friends knew a very different Tom Weiskopf from the 'Towering Inferno' of his public image. They understood that his occasional anger on the course was not the product of a bad temper so much as disappointment with himself for failing to reach the high standards he had set for himself, that his outspoken comments at times were expressions of an innate honesty from a man who could not dissemble or compromise his beliefs. Weiskopf's swing surely qualified for the adjective majestic, not cramped in the manner of many golfers of 6′ 3″, but deriving from a full turn of his athletic frame with a measured tempo which packed a colossal punch at impact. When Weiskopf applied himself heart and soul to golf he was virtually invincible. During one eight-week period in 1973, following the death of his father when he felt that he had frittered away his talent and wanted to make an act of homage to his parent's aspirations, he won five tournaments. The last of them was the Open championship at Troon where Weiskopf played an almost flawless final round of controlled power. He went on winning, inevitably so with the resources at his command, but his motivation wavered. Like a few others before him, he scrutinised his career, questioning whether an essentially frivolous activity such as golf was a fit pursuit to which an adult should devote his life. He did not take himself off to a monastery, like the South African Retief Waltman or the Irish pro Sean Hunt when they were afflicted by doubts. Weiskopf took refuge in the wilderness with his hunting rifle. He hated to play at less than his best but he simply could not generate enough interest to give of his best. One year he even passed up his chance to represent his country in the Ryder Cup match, which most professionals rank among the highest honours the game can bestow, and went hunting instead. In 1979 he went into a three-year victory drought and, although he came back with two more tournament wins, his heart was clearly not in the game. So one of the greatest of post-war golfers faded from the scene, leaving a record which did less than justice to an exceptional talent.

*Open champion 1973. Member of two Ryder Cup teams and
one World Cup team.*

Mike Francis

FUZZY ZOELLER

b. New Albany, Indiana, 11 November, 1951

The first point to dispose of is that name. His birth certificate records him as Frank Urban Zoeller, hence the initials F.U.Z., hence Fuzzy, nothing to do with the permanent wave which he affected to fit the nickname but precisely the reverse. His family home was on a golf course in Indiana and he first started knocking a ball about at the age of three, as naturally as kids who live by a lake learn to swim. Two years later he was entered for his first tournament. Zoeller was besotted by sports of all kind and it was while playing high school basketball that he received the back injury which was to plague his golfing career, sentencing him to a regime of pain-killing drugs and corsets. Fortunately he was blessed with an irrepressible nature and the disability, although incapacitating at times, did not deter him. He would be the last man to claim a place in any list of great golfers, persisting in his self-appraisal as an honest trier who got lucky even after he had won the Masters and the US Open. There may have been an element of luck about his victory in the 1979 Masters but it was the bad luck which attended leader Ed Sneed in dropping strokes from good shots over the closing holes which put Zoeller into a play-off. There was nothing lucky about his second classic win, the 1984 US Open championship at Winged Foot. Zoeller fought out an absorbing duel with the Australian Greg Norman, off-setting the damages of a faltering swing in the final round by putting of uncanny accuracy. Norman was playing in the group ahead on the last day and when a huge cheer went up from the crowds around the 18th green Zoeller, waiting down the fairway, thought the applause signalled a birdie which must seal Norman's victory. In fact the shout was for the saving of a most improbable par after Norman had seemingly lost his chance. In keeping with his sportsmanlike and happy-go-lucky nature, Zoeller waved a white towel in token of surrender, a premature gesture as it turned out. In the play-off Zoeller won easily against a jaded Norman. In an age when professional golf is becoming increasingly solemn and sullen, Zoeller's cheery nature is a timely reminder that golf, even with millions of dollars at stake, is a game, a pursuit designed for enjoyment.

US Open champion 1984. Masters champion 1979. Member of 1983 Ryder Cup team.

Rodger Towers

ACKNOWLEDGEMENTS

The Pictures
The Lord's Taverners and the artists gratefully acknowledge the generous help given to them by Sport & General (and librarian Nick Pearce) who provided photographic references for most of the portraits in the book.

They would also like to thank Press Association Photos for supplying material on Julius Boros, Doug Ford, Don January, Gene Littler and Fuzzy Zoeller; Lawrence Levy for his photograph of Tommy Bolt; and Peter Dazeley for his photographs of Peter Alliss and Byron Nelson.

Finally their thanks go to Bill Robertson, editor of *Golf Illustrated*, who kindly allowed the artists access to the magazine's extensive photo collection for the purposes of research.

The Words
Many sources of reference are required to gather and confirm information for a work of this nature. However, special acknowledgement is due to *The Price World of Golf* by Charlie Price, *The Shell International Encyclopedia of Golf, Benson and Hedges Golfer's Handbook*, and archive material of the United States Golf Association, the Royal and Ancient golf club of St Andrews, the Professional Golfers' Associations of the United States and of Great Britain, and the library of *Golf Digest* magazine.